Harvard Business Review

ON

BUSINESS AND THE
ENVIRONMENT

THE HARVARD BUSINESS REVIEW PAPERBACK SERIES

The series is designed to bring today's managers and professionals the fundamental information they need to stay competitive in a fast-moving world. From the preeminent thinkers whose work has defined an entire field to the rising stars who will redefine the way we think about business, here are the leading minds and landmark ideas that have established the *Harvard Business Review* as required reading for ambitious businesspeople in organizations around the globe.

Other books in the series:

Harvard Business Review on Brand Management
Harvard Business Review on Breakthrough Thinking
Harvard Business Review on the Business Value of IT
Harvard Business Review on Change
Harvard Business Review on Corporate Governance
Harvard Business Review on Corporate Strategy
Harvard Business Review on Crisis Management
Harvard Business Review on Effective Communication
Harvard Business Review on Entrepreneurship
Harvard Business Review on Knowledge Management
Harvard Business Review on Leadership
Harvard Business Review on Managing High-Tech Industries
Harvard Business Review on Managing People
Harvard Business Review on Managing Uncertainty
Harvard Business Review on Managing the Value Chain
Harvard Business Review on Measuring Corporate Performance
Harvard Business Review on Negotiation and Conflict Resolution
Harvard Business Review on Nonprofits
Harvard Business Review on Strategies for Growth

Harvard
Business
Review

ON

BUSINESS AND THE
ENVIRONMENT

A HARVARD BUSINESS REVIEW PAPERBACK

The *Harvard Business Review* articles in this collection are available as individual reprints. Discounts apply to quantity purchases. For information and ordering, please contact Customer Service, Harvard Business School Publishing, Boston, MA 02163. Telephone: (617) 783-7500 or (800) 988-0886, 8 A.M. to 6 P.M. Eastern Time, Monday through Friday. Fax: (617) 783-7555, 24 hours a day. E-mail: custserv@hbsp.harvard.edu.

Library of Congress Cataloging-in-Publication Data
Harvard business review on business and the environment.
    p.   cm. — (The Harvard business review paperback series)
    Includes index.
    ISBN 1-57851-233-6 (alk. paper)
    1. Industrial management—Environmental aspects.   2. Green movement.   3. Social responsibility of business.   4. Environmental protection.   I. Harvard business review.   II. Title: Business and the environment.   III. Series.
HD69.P6H373   2000
658.4'08—dc21   99-28451
                                                  CIP

The paper used in this publication meets the requirements of the American National Standard for Permanence of Paper for Publications and Documents in Libraries and Archives Z39.48-1992.

Contents

Harvard
Business
Review

ON

BUSINESS AND THE
ENVIRONMENT

A Road Map for Natural Capitalism

AMORY B. LOVINS, L. HUNTER LOVINS,
AND PAUL HAWKEN

Executive Summary

NO ONE WOULD RUN a business without accounting for its capital outlays. Yet most companies overlook one major capital component—the value of the earth's ecosystem services. It is a staggering omission; recent calculations place the value of the earth's total ecosystem services—water storage, atmosphere regulation, climate control, and so on—at $33 trillion a year.

Not accounting for those costs has led to waste on a grand scale. But now a few farsighted companies are finding powerful business opportunities in conserving resources on a similarly grand scale. They are embarking on a journey toward "natural capitalism," a journey that comprises four major shifts in business practices.

The first stage involves dramatically increasing the productivity of natural resources, stretching them as much as 100 times further than they do today. In the second stage, companies adopt closed-loop production systems that yield no waste or toxicity. The third stage requires a fundamental change of business model—from one of selling products to one of delivering services. For example, a manufacturer would sell lighting services rather than lightbulbs, thus benefiting the seller and customer for developing extremely efficient, durable lightbulbs. The last stage involves reinvesting in natural capital to restore, sustain, and expand the planet's ecosystem.

Because natural capitalism is both necessary and profitable, it will subsume traditional industrialism, the authors argue, just as industrialism subsumed agrarianism. And the companies that are furthest down the road will have the competitive edge.

ON SEPTEMBER 16, 1991, a small group of scientists was sealed inside Biosphere II, a glittering 3.2-acre glass and metal dome in Oracle, Arizona. Two years later, when the radical attempt to replicate the earth's main ecosystems in miniature ended, the engineered environment was dying. The gaunt researchers had survived only because fresh air had been pumped in. Despite $200 million worth of elaborate equipment, Biosphere II had failed to generate breathable air, drinkable water, and adequate food for just eight people. Yet Biosphere I, the planet we all inhabit, effortlessly performs those tasks every day for 6 billion of us.

Disturbingly, Biosphere I is now itself at risk. The earth's ability to sustain life, and therefore economic activity, is threatened by the way we extract, process, transport, and dispose of a vast flow of resources—

some 220 billion tons a year, or more than 20 times the average American's body weight every day. With dangerously narrow focus, our industries look only at the exploitable resources of the earth's ecosystems—its oceans, forests, and plains—and not at the larger services that those systems provide for free. Resources and ecosystem services both come from the earth—even from the same biological systems—but they're two different things. Forests, for instance, not only produce the resource of wood fiber but also provide such ecosystem services as water storage, habitat, and regulation of the atmosphere and climate. Yet companies that earn income from harvesting the wood fiber resource often do so in ways that damage the forest's ability to carry out its other vital tasks.

Unfortunately, the cost of destroying ecosystem services becomes apparent only when the services start to break down. In China's Yangtze basin in 1998, for example, deforestation triggered flooding that killed 3,700 people, dislocated 223 million, and inundated 60 million acres of cropland. That $30 billion disaster forced a logging moratorium and a $12 billion crash program of reforestation.

Some very simple changes to the way we run our businesses can yield startling benefits for today's shareholders and for future generations.

The reason companies (and governments) are so prodigal with ecosystem services is that the value of those services doesn't appear on the business balance sheet. But that's a staggering omission. The economy, after all, is embedded in the environment. Recent calculations published in the journal *Nature* conservatively estimate the value of all the earth's ecosystem services to be at least $33 trillion a year. That's close to the gross world product, and it implies a capitalized book value on the order of half a quadrillion dollars. What's more, for most of these services, there is no known substitute at any price, and we can't live without them.

This article puts forward a new approach not only for protecting the biosphere but also for improving profits and competitiveness. Some very simple changes to the way we run our businesses, built on advanced techniques for making resources more productive, can yield startling benefits both for today's shareholders and for future generations.

This approach is called *natural capitalism* because it's what capitalism might become if its largest category of capital—the "natural capital" of ecosystem services—were properly valued. The journey to natural capitalism involves four major shifts in business practices, all vitally interlinked:

Dramatically increase the productivity of natural resources. Reducing the wasteful and destructive flow of resources from depletion to pollution represents a major business opportunity. Through fundamental changes in both production design and technology, farsighted companies are developing ways to make natural resources—energy, minerals, water, forests—stretch 5, 10, even 100 times further than they do today. These major resource savings often yield higher profits than small resource savings

Saving a large fraction of resources can actually cost less than saving a small fraction of resources. This is the concept of expanding returns.

do—or even saving no resources at all would—and not only pay for themselves over time but in many cases reduce initial capital investments.

Shift to biologically inspired production models. Natural capitalism seeks not merely to reduce waste but to eliminate the very concept of waste. In closed-loop production systems, modeled on nature's designs, every output either is returned harmlessly to the ecosystem as a nutrient, like compost, or becomes an input for manufacturing another product. Such systems can often be designed to eliminate the use of toxic materials, which can hamper nature's ability to reprocess materials.

Move to a solutions-based business model The business model of traditional manufacturing rests on the sale of goods. In the new model, value is instead delivered as a flow of services—providing illumination, for example, rather than selling lightbulbs. This model entails a new perception of value, a move from the acquisition of goods as a measure of affluence to one where well-being is measured by the continuous satisfaction of changing expectations for quality, utility, and performance. The new relationship aligns the interests of providers and customers in ways that reward them for implementing the first two innovations of natural capitalism—resource productivity and closed-loop manufacturing.

Reinvest in natural capital. Ultimately, business must restore, sustain, and expand the planet's ecosystems so that they can produce their vital services and biological resources even more abundantly. Pressures to do so are mounting as human needs expand, the costs engendered by deteriorating ecosystems rise, and the environmental awareness of consumers increases. Fortunately, these pressures all create business value.

Natural capitalism is not motivated by a current scarcity of natural resources. Indeed, although many biological resources, like fish, are becoming scarce, most mined resources, such as copper and oil, seem ever more abundant. Indices of average commodity prices are at 28-year lows, thanks partly to powerful extractive technologies, which are often subsidized and whose damage to natural capital remains unaccounted for. Yet even despite these artificially low prices, using resources manyfold more productively can now be so profitable that pioneering companies—large and small—have already embarked on the journey toward natural capitalism.[1]

Still the question arises—if large resource savings are available and profitable, why haven't they all been captured already? The answer is simple: scores of common practices in both the private and public sectors systematically reward companies for wasting natural resources and penalize them for boosting resource productivity. For example, most companies expense their consumption of raw materials through the income statement but pass resource-saving investment through the balance sheet. That distortion makes it more tax efficient to waste fuel than to invest in improving fuel efficiency. In short, even though the road seems clear, the compass that companies use to direct their journey is broken. Later we'll look in more detail at some of the obstacles to resource productivity—and some of the important business opportunities they reveal. But first, let's map the route toward natural capitalism.

Dramatically Increase the Productivity of Natural Resources

In the first stage of a company's journey toward natural capitalism, it strives to wring out the waste of energy, water, materials, and other resources throughout its production systems and other operations. There are two main ways companies can do this at a profit. First, they can adopt a fresh approach to design that considers industrial systems as a whole rather than part by part. Second, companies can replace old industrial technologies with new ones, particularly with those based on natural processes and materials.

IMPLEMENTING WHOLE-SYSTEM DESIGN

Inventor Edwin Land once remarked that "people who seem to have had a new idea have often simply stopped having an old idea." This is particularly true when designing for resource savings. The old idea is one of diminishing returns—the greater the resource saving, the higher the cost. But that old idea is giving way to the new idea that bigger savings can cost less—that saving a large fraction of resources can actually cost less than saving a small fraction of resources. This is the concept of expanding returns, and it governs much of the revolutionary thinking behind whole-system design. Lean manufacturing is an example of whole-system thinking that has helped many companies dramatically reduce such forms of waste as lead times, defect rates, and inventory. Applying whole-system thinking to the productivity of natural resources can achieve even more.

Consider Interface Corporation, a leading maker of materials for commercial interiors. In its new Shanghai carpet factory, a liquid had to be circulated through a standard pumping loop similar to those used in nearly all industries. A top European company designed the system to use pumps requiring a total of 95 horsepower. But before construction began, Interface's engineer, Jan Schilham, realized that two embarrassingly simple design changes would cut that power requirement to only 7 horsepower—a 92% reduction. His redesigned system cost less to build, involved no new technology, and worked better in all respects.

Interface's engineer realized that two embarrassingly simple design changes would cut power requirements by 92%.

What two design changes achieved this 12-fold saving in pumping power? First, Schilham chose fatter-than-usual pipes, which create much less friction than thin pipes do and therefore need far less pumping energy. The original designer had chosen thin pipes because, according to the textbook method, the extra cost of fatter ones wouldn't be justified by the pumping energy that they would save. This standard design trade-off optimizes the pipes by themselves but "pessimizes" the larger system. Schilham optimized the *whole* system by counting not only the higher capital cost of the fatter pipes but also the *lower* capital cost of the smaller pumping equipment that would be needed. The pumps, motors, motor controls, and electrical components could all be much smaller because there'd be less friction to overcome. Capital cost would fall far more for the smaller equipment than it would rise for the fatter pipe. Choosing big pipes and small pumps—rather than small pipes and big pumps—would therefore make the whole system cost less to build, even before counting its future energy savings.

Schilham's second innovation was to reduce the friction even more by making the pipes short and straight rather than long and crooked. He did this by laying out the pipes first, *then* positioning the various tanks, boilers, and other equipment that they connected. Designers normally locate the production equipment in arbitrary positions and then have a pipe fitter connect everything. Awkward placement forces the pipes to make numerous bends that greatly increase friction. The pipe fitters don't mind: they're paid by the hour, they profit from the extra pipes and fittings, and they don't pay for the oversized pumps or inflated electric bills. In addition to reducing those four kinds of costs, Schilham's short, straight pipes were easier to insulate, saving an extra 70 kilowatts of heat loss and repaying the insulation's cost in three months.

This small example has big implications for two reasons. First, pumping is the largest application of motors, and motors use three-quarters of all industrial electricity. Second, the lessons are very widely relevant. Interface's pumping loop shows how simple changes in design mentality can yield huge resource savings and returns on investment. This isn't rocket science; often it's just a rediscovery of good Victorian engineering principles that have been lost because of specialization.

Whole-system thinking can help managers find small changes that lead to big savings that are cheap, free, or even better than free (because they make the whole system cheaper to build). They can do this because often the right investment in one part of the system can produce multiple benefits throughout the system. For example, companies would gain 18 distinct economic benefits—of which direct energy savings is only one—if they switched from ordinary motors to premium-efficiency motors or from ordinary lighting ballasts (the transformer-like boxes that control fluorescent lamps) to electronic ballasts that automatically dim the lamps to match available daylight. If everyone in America integrated these and other selected technologies into all existing motor and lighting systems in an optimal way, the nation's $220-billion-a-year electric bill would be cut in half. The after-tax return on investing in these changes would in most cases exceed 100% per year.

The profits from saving electricity could be increased even further if companies also incorporated the best off-the-shelf improvements into their building structure and their office, heating, cooling, and other equipment. Overall, such changes could cut national electricity consumption by at least 75% and produce returns of around 100% a year on the investments made. More important, because workers would be more comfortable, better able to see, and less fatigued by noise, their productivity and the quality of their output would rise. Eight recent case studies of people working in well-designed, energy-efficient buildings measured labor productivity gains of 6% to 16%. Since a typical office pays about 100 times as much for people as it does for energy, this increased productivity in people is worth about 6 to 16 times as much as eliminating the entire energy bill.

Energy-saving, productivity-enhancing improvements can often be achieved at even lower cost by piggybacking them onto the periodic renovations that all buildings and factories need. A recent proposal for reallocating the normal 20-year renovation budget for a standard 200,000-square-foot glass-clad office tower near Chicago, Illinois, shows the potential of whole-system design. The proposal suggested replacing the aging glazing system with a new kind of window that lets in nearly six times more daylight than the old sun-blocking glass units. The new windows would reduce the flow of heat and noise four times better than traditional windows do. So even though the glass costs slightly more, the overall cost of the renovation would be reduced because the windows would let in cool, glare-free daylight that, when combined with more efficient lighting and office equipment, would reduce the need for air-conditioning by 75%. Installing a fourfold more efficient, but fourfold smaller, air-conditioning system would cost $200,000 less than giving the old system its normal 20-year renovation. The $200,000 saved would, in turn, pay for the extra cost of the new windows and other improvements. This whole-system approach to renovation would not only save 75% of the building's total energy use, it would also greatly improve the building's comfort and marketability. Yet it would cost essentially the same as the normal renovation. There are about 100,000 twenty-year-old glass office towers in the United States that are ripe for such improvement.

Major gains in resource productivity require that the right steps be taken in the right order. Small changes made at the downstream end of a process often create far larger savings further upstream. In almost any industry that uses a pumping system, for example, saving one unit of liquid flow or friction in an exit pipe saves about ten units of fuel, cost, and pollution at the power station.

Of course, the original reduction in flow itself can bring direct benefits, which are often the reason changes are made in the first place. In the 1980s, while California's industry grew 30%, for example, its water use was cut by 30%, largely to avoid increased wastewater fees.

But the resulting reduction in pumping energy (and the roughly tenfold larger saving in power-plant fuel and pollution) delivered bonus savings that were at the time largely unanticipated.

To see how downstream cuts in resource consumption can create huge savings upstream, consider how reducing the use of wood fiber disproportionately reduces the pressure to cut down forests. In round numbers, half of all harvested wood fiber is used for such structural products as lumber; the other half is used for paper and cardboard. In both cases, the biggest leverage comes from reducing the amount of the retail product used. If it takes, for example, three pounds of harvested trees to produce one pound of product, then saving one pound of product will save three pounds of trees—plus all the environmental damage avoided by not having to cut them down in the first place.

In an experiment at its Swiss headquarters, Dow Europe cut office paper flow by about 30% in six weeks simply by discouraging unneeded information.

The easiest savings come from not using paper that's unwanted or unneeded. In an experiment at its Swiss headquarters, for example, Dow Europe cut office paper flow by about 30% in six weeks simply by discouraging unneeded information. For instance, mailing lists were eliminated and senders of memos got back receipts indicating whether each recipient had wanted the information. Taking those and other small steps, Dow was also able to increase labor productivity by a similar proportion because people could focus on what they really needed to read. Similarly, Danish hearing-aid maker Oticon saved upwards of 30% of its paper as a by-product of redesigning its business processes to produce better decisions faster. Setting the default on office printers and copiers to double-sided mode reduced AT&T's paper costs by about 15%. Recently developed copiers and printers can even strip off old toner and printer ink, permitting each sheet to be reused about ten times.

Further savings can come from using thinner but stronger and more opaque paper, and from designing packaging more thoughtfully. In a 30-month effort at reducing such waste, Johnson & Johnson saved 2,750 tons of packaging, 1,600 tons of paper, $2.8 million, and at least 330 acres of forest annually. The downstream savings in paper use are

We could use wood fiber so much more productively that, in principle, the entire world's wood fiber needs could probably be met by an intensive tree farm about the size of Iowa.

multiplied by the savings further upstream, as less need for paper products (or less need for fiber to make each product) translates into less raw paper, less raw paper means less pulp, and less pulp requires fewer trees to be harvested from the forest. Recycling paper and substituting alternative fibers such as wheat straw will save even more.

Comparable savings can be achieved for the wood fiber used in structural products. Pacific Gas and Electric, for example, sponsored an innovative design developed by Davis Energy Group that used engineered wood products to reduce the amount of wood needed in a stud wall for a typical tract house by more than 70%. These walls were stronger, cheaper, more stable, and insulated twice as well. Using them enabled the designers to eliminate heating and cooling equipment in a climate where temperatures range from freezing to 113°F. Eliminating the equipment made the whole house much less expensive both to build and to run while still maintaining high levels of comfort. Taken together, these and many other savings in the paper and construction industries could make our use of wood fiber so much more productive that, in principle, the entire world's present wood fiber needs could probably be met by an intensive tree farm about the size of Iowa.

ADOPTING INNOVATIVE TECHNOLOGIES

Implementing whole-system design goes hand in hand with introducing alternative, environmentally friendly technologies. Many of these are already available and profitable but not widely known. Some, like the "designer catalysts" that are transforming the chemical industry, are already runaway successes. Others are still making their way to market, delayed by cultural rather than by economic or technical barriers.

The automobile industry is particularly ripe for technological change. After a century of development, motorcar technology is showing signs of age. Only 1% of the energy consumed by today's cars is actually used to move the driver: only 15% to 20% of the power generated by burning gasoline reaches the wheels (the rest is lost in the engine and drivetrain) and 95% of the resulting propulsion moves the car, not the driver. The industry's infrastructure is hugely expensive and inefficient. Its convergent products compete for narrow niches in saturated core markets at commoditylike prices. Auto making is capital intensive, and product cycles are long. It is profitable in good years but subject to large losses in bad years. Like the typewriter industry just before the advent of personal computers, it is vulnerable to displacement by something completely different.

Enter the Hypercar. Since 1993, when Rocky Mountain Institute placed this automotive concept in the public domain, several dozen current and potential auto manufacturers have committed billions of dollars to its development and commercialization. The Hypercar integrates the best existing technologies to reduce the consumption of fuel as much as 85% and the amount of materials used up to 90% by introducing four main innovations.

First, making the vehicle out of advanced polymer composites, chiefly carbon fiber, reduces its weight by two-thirds while maintaining crashworthiness. Second, aerodynamic design and better tires reduce air resistance by as much as 70% and rolling resistance by up to 80%. Together, these innovations save about two-thirds of the fuel. Third, 30% to 50% of the remaining fuel is saved by using a "hybrid-electric" drive. In such a system, the wheels are turned by electric motors whose power is made onboard by a small engine or turbine, or even more efficiently by a fuel cell. The fuel cell generates electricity directly by chemically combining stored hydrogen with oxygen, producing pure hot water as its only by-product. Interactions between the small, clean, efficient power source and the ultralight, low-drag auto body then further reduce the weight, cost, and complexity of both. Fourth, much of the traditional hardware—from transmissions and differentials to gauges and certain parts of the suspension—can be replaced by electronics controlled with highly integrated, customizable, and upgradable software.

These technologies make it feasible to manufacture pollution-free, high-performance cars, sport utilities, pickup trucks, and vans that get 80 to 200 miles per gallon (or its energy equivalent in other fuels). These improvements will not require any compromise in quality or utility. Fuel savings will not come from making the vehicles small, sluggish, unsafe, or unaffordable, nor will they depend on government fuel taxes, mandates, or subsidies. Rather, Hypercars will succeed for the same reason that people buy compact discs instead of phonograph records: the CD is a superior product that redefines market expectations. From the manufacturers' perspective, Hypercars will cut cycle times, capital needs, body part counts, and assembly effort and space by as much as tenfold. Early adopters will have a huge competitive advantage—which is why dozens of corporations, including most automakers, are now racing to bring Hypercar-like products to market.[2]

In the long term, the Hypercar will transform industries other than automobiles. It will displace about an eighth of the steel market directly and most of the rest eventually, as carbon fiber becomes far cheaper. Hypercars and their cousins could ultimately save as much oil as OPEC now sells. Indeed, oil may well become uncompetitive as a fuel long before it becomes scarce and costly. Similar challenges face the coal and electricity industries because the development of the Hypercar is likely to accelerate greatly the commercialization of inexpensive hydrogen fuel cells. These fuel cells will help shift power production from centralized coal-fired and nuclear power stations to networks of decentralized, small-scale generators. In fact, fuel-cell-powered Hypercars could themselves be part of these networks. They'd be, in effect, 20-kilowatt power plants on wheels. Given that cars are left parked—that is, unused—more than 95% of the time, these Hypercars could be plugged into a grid and could then sell back enough electricity to repay as much as half the predicted cost of leasing them. A national Hypercar fleet could ultimately have five to ten times the generating capacity of the national electric grid.

As radical as it sounds, the Hypercar is not an isolated case. Similar ideas are emerging in such industries as chemicals, semiconductors, general manufacturing, transportation, water and waste-water treatment, agriculture, forestry, energy, real estate, and urban design.

Only about 1% of all materials mobilized to serve America is actually made into products and still in use six months after sale.

For example, the amount of carbon dioxide released for each microchip manufactured can be reduced almost 100-fold through improvements that are now profitable or soon will be.

Some of the most striking developments come from emulating nature's techniques. In her book, *Biomimicry*, Janine Benyus points out that spiders convert digested crickets and flies into silk that's as strong as Kevlar without the need for boiling sulfuric acid and high-temperature extruders. Using no furnaces, abalone can convert seawater into an inner shell twice as tough as our best ceramics. Trees turn sunlight, water, soil, and air into cellulose, a sugar stronger than nylon but one-fourth as dense. They then bind it into wood, a natural composite with a higher bending strength than concrete, aluminum alloy, or steel. We may never become as skillful as spiders, abalone, or trees, but smart designers are already realizing that nature's environmentally benign chemistry offers attractive alternatives to industrial brute force.

Whether through better design or through new technologies, reducing waste represents a vast business opportunity. The U.S. economy is not even 10% as energy efficient as the laws of physics allow. Just the energy thrown off as waste heat by U.S. power stations equals the total energy use of Japan. Materials efficiency is even worse: only about 1% of all the materials mobilized to serve America is actually made into products and still in use six months after sale. In every sector, there are opportunities for reducing the amount of resources that go into a production process, the steps required to run that process, and the amount of pollution generated and by-products discarded at the end. These all represent avoidable costs and hence profits to be won.

Redesign Production According to Biological Models

In the second stage on the journey to natural capitalism, companies use closed-loop manufacturing to create new products and processes that can totally prevent waste. This plus more efficient production processes could cut companies' long-term materials requirements by more than 90% in most sectors.

The central principle of closed-loop manufacturing, as architect Paul Bierman-Lytle of the engineering firm CH2M Hill puts it, is "waste equals food." Every output of manufacturing should be either composted into natural nutrients or remanufactured into technical nutrients— that is, it should be returned to the ecosystem or recycled for further production. Closed-loop production systems are designed to eliminate any materials that incur disposal costs, especially toxic ones, because the alternative—isolating them to prevent harm to natural systems—tends to be costly and risky. Indeed, meeting EPA and OSHA standards by eliminating harmful materials often makes a manufacturing process cost less than the hazardous process it replaced. Motorola, for example, formerly used chlorofluorocarbons for cleaning printed circuit boards after soldering. When CFCs were outlawed because they destroy stratospheric ozone, Motorola at first explored such alternatives as orange-peel terpenes. But it turned out to be even cheaper—and to produce a better product—to redesign the whole soldering process so that it needed no cleaning operations or cleaning materials at all.

Closed-loop manufacturing is more than just a theory. The U.S. remanufacturing industry in 1996 reported revenues of $53 billion—more than consumer-durables manufacturing (appliances; furniture; audio, video, farm, and garden equipment). Xerox, whose bottom line has swelled by $700 million from remanufacturing, expects to save another $1 billion just by remanufacturing its new, entirely reusable or recyclable line of "green" photocopiers. What's more, policy makers in some countries are already taking steps to encourage industry to think along these lines. German law, for example, makes many manufacturers responsible for their products forever, and Japan is following suit.

Combining closed-loop manufacturing with resource efficiency is especially powerful. DuPont, for example, gets much of its polyester industrial film back from customers after they use it and recycles it into new film. DuPont also makes its polyester film ever stronger and thinner so it uses less material and costs less to make. Yet because the film performs better, customers are willing to pay more for it. As DuPont chairman Jack Krol noted in 1997, "Our ability to continually improve the inherent properties [of our films] enables this process [of developing more productive materials, at lower cost, and higher profits] to go on indefinitely."

Interface is leading the way to this next frontier of industrial ecology. While its competitors are "down cycling" nylon-and-PVC-based carpet into less valuable carpet backing, Interface has invented a new floor-covering material called Solenium, which can be completely remanufactured into identical new product. This fundamental innovation emerged from a clean-sheet redesign. Executives at Interface didn't ask how they could sell more carpet of the familiar kind; they asked how they could create a dream product that would best meet their customers' needs while protecting and nourishing natural capital.

Solenium lasts four times longer and uses 40% less material than ordinary carpets—an 86% reduction in materials intensity. What's more, Solenium is free of chlorine and other toxic materials, is virtually stain-proof, doesn't grow mildew, can easily be cleaned with water, and offers aesthetic advantages over traditional carpets. It's so superior in every respect that Interface doesn't market it as an environmental product—just a better one.

Solenium is only one part of Interface's drive to eliminate every form of waste. Chairman Ray C. Anderson defines waste as "any measurable input that does not produce customer value," and he considers all inputs to be waste until shown otherwise. Between 1994 and 1998, this zero-waste approach led to a systematic treasure hunt that helped to keep resource inputs constant while revenues rose by $200 million. Indeed, $67 million of the revenue increase can be directly attributed to the company's 60% reduction in landfill waste.

Subsequently, president Charlie Eitel expanded the definition of waste to include all fossil fuel inputs, and now many customers are eager to buy products from the company's recently opened solar-powered carpet factory. Interface's green strategy has not only won plaudits from environmentalists, it has also proved a remarkably successful business strategy. Between 1993 and 1998, revenue has more than doubled, profits have more than tripled, and the number of employees has increased by 73%.

Change the Business Model

In addition to its drive to eliminate waste, Interface has made a fundamental shift in its business model—the third stage on the journey toward natural capitalism. The company has realized that clients want to walk on and look at carpets—but not necessarily to own them. Traditionally, broadloom carpets in office buildings are replaced every decade because some portions look worn out. When that happens, companies suffer the disruption of shutting down their offices and removing their furniture. Billions of pounds of carpets are removed each year and sent to landfills, where they will last up to 20,000 years. To escape this unproductive and wasteful cycle, Interface is transforming itself from a company that sells and fits carpets into one that provides floor-covering services.

Under its Evergreen Lease, Interface no longer sells carpets but rather leases a floor-covering service for a monthly fee, accepting responsibility for keeping the carpet fresh and clean. Monthly inspections detect and replace worn carpet tiles. Since at most 20% of an area typically shows at least 80% of the wear, replacing only the worn parts reduces the consumption of carpeting material by about 80%. It also minimizes the disruption that customers experience—worn tiles are seldom found under furniture. Finally, for the customer, leasing carpets can provide a tax advantage by turning a capital expenditure into a tax-deductible expense. The result: the customer gets cheaper and better services that cost the supplier far less to produce. Indeed, the energy saved from not producing a whole new carpet is in itself enough to produce all the carpeting that the new business model requires. Taken together, the 5-fold savings in carpeting material that Interface achieves through the Evergreen Lease and the 7-fold materials savings achieved through the use of Solenium deliver a stunning 35-fold reduction in the flow of materials needed to sustain a superior floor-covering service. Remanufacturing, and even making carpet initially from renewable materials, can then reduce the extraction of virgin resources essentially to the company's goal of zero.

Elevator giant Schindler prefers leasing vertical transportation services to selling elevators because leasing lets it capture the savings from its elevators' lower energy and maintenance costs.

Interface's shift to a service-leasing business reflects a fundamental change from the basic model of most manufacturing companies, which still look on their businesses as machines for producing and selling products. The more products sold, the better—at least for the company, if not always for the customer or the earth. But any model that wastes natural resources also wastes money. Ultimately, that model will be unable to compete with a service model that emphasizes solving problems and building long-term relationships with customers rather than making and selling products. The shift to what James Womack of the Lean Enterprise Institute calls a "solutions economy" will almost always improve customer value *and* providers' bottom lines because it aligns both parties' interests, offering rewards for doing more and better with less.

Interface is not alone. Elevator giant Schindler, for example, prefers leasing vertical transportation services to selling elevators because leasing lets it capture the savings from its elevators' lower energy and maintenance costs. Dow Chemical and Safety-Kleen prefer leasing dissolving services to selling solvents because they can reuse the same solvent scores of times, reducing costs. United Technologies' Carrier division, the world's largest manufacturer of air conditioners, is shifting its mission from selling air conditioners to leasing comfort. Making its air conditioners more durable and efficient may compromise future equipment sales, but it provides what customers want and will pay for—better comfort at lower cost. But Carrier is going even further. It's starting to team up with other companies to make buildings more efficient so that they need less air-conditioning, or even none at all, to yield the same level of comfort. Carrier will get paid to provide the agreed-upon level of comfort, however that's delivered. Higher profits will come from providing better solutions rather than from selling more equipment. Since comfort with little or no air-conditioning (via better building design) works better and costs less than comfort with copious air-conditioning, Carrier is smart to capture this opportunity itself before its competitors do. As they say at 3M: "We'd rather eat our *own* lunch, thank you."

The shift to a service business model promises benefits not just to participating businesses but to the entire economy as well. Womack points out that by helping customers reduce their need for capital goods such as carpets or elevators, and by rewarding suppliers for extending and maximizing asset values rather than for churning them, adoption of the service model will reduce the volatility in the turnover of capital goods that lies at the heart of the business cycle. That would significantly reduce the overall volatility of the world's economy. At present, the producers of capital goods face feast or famine because the buying decisions of households and corporations are extremely sensitive to fluctuating income. But in a continuous-flow-of-services economy, those swings would be greatly reduced, bringing a welcome stability to businesses. Excess capacity—another form of waste and source of risk—need no longer be retained for meeting peak demand. The result of adopting the new model would be an economy in which we grow and get richer by using less and become stronger by being leaner and more stable.

Reinvest in Natural Capital

The foundation of textbook capitalism is the prudent reinvestment of earnings in productive capital. Natural capitalists who have dramatically raised their resource productivity, closed their loops, and shifted to a solutions-based business model have one key task remaining. They must reinvest in restoring, sustaining, and expanding the most important form of capital— their own natural habitat and biological resource base.

This was not always so important. Until recently, business could ignore damage to the ecosystem because it didn't affect production and didn't increase costs. But that situation is changing. In 1998 alone, violent weather displaced 300 million people and caused upwards of $90 billion worth of damage, representing more weather-related destruction than was reported through the entire decade of the 1980s. The increase in damage is strongly linked to deforestation and climate change, factors that accelerate the frequency and severity of natural disasters and are the consequences of inefficient industrialization. If the flow of services from industrial systems is to be sustained or increased in the future for a growing population, the vital flow of services from living systems will have to be maintained or increased as well. Without reinvestment in natural capital, shortages of ecosystem services are likely to become the limiting factor to prosperity in the next century. When a manufacturer realizes that a supplier of key components is overextended and running behind on deliveries, it takes immediate action lest its own production lines come to a halt. The ecosystem is a supplier of key components for the life of the planet, and it is now falling behind on its orders.

Failure to protect and reinvest in natural capital can also hit a company's revenues indirectly. Many companies are discovering that public perceptions of environmental responsibility, or its lack thereof, affect sales. MacMillan Bloedel, targeted by environmental activists as an emblematic clear-cutter and chlorine user, lost 5% of its sales almost overnight when dropped as a U.K. supplier by Scott Paper and Kimberly-Clark. Numerous case studies show that companies leading the way in implementing changes that help protect the environment tend to gain disproportionate advantage, while companies perceived as irresponsible lose their franchise, their legitimacy, and their shirts. Even businesses that claim to be committed to the concept of sustainable development but whose strategy is seen as mistaken, like Monsanto, are encountering stiffening public resistance to their products. Not surprisingly, University of Oregon business professor Michael Russo, along with many other analysts, has found that a strong environmental rating is "a consistent predictor of profitability."

The pioneering corporations that have made reinvestments in natural capital are starting to see some interesting paybacks. The independent power producer AES, for example, has long pursued a policy of planting trees to offset the carbon emissions of its power plants. That ethical stance, once thought quixotic, now looks like a smart investment because a dozen brokers are now starting to create markets in carbon reduction. Similarly, certification by the Forest Stewardship Council of certain sustainably grown and harvested products has given Collins Pine the extra profit margins that enabled its U.S. manufacturing operations to survive brutal competition. Taking an even longer view, Swiss Re and other European reinsurers are seeking to cut their storm-damage losses by pressing for international public policy to protect the climate and by investing in climate-safe technologies that also promise good profits. Yet most companies still do not realize that a vibrant ecological web underpins their survival and their business success. Enriching natural capital is not just a public good—it is vital to every company's longevity.

It turns out that changing industrial processes so that they actually replenish and magnify the stock of natural capital can prove especially profitable because nature does the production; people need just step back and let life flourish. Industries that directly harvest living resources, such as forestry, farming, and fishing, offer the most suggestive examples. Here are three:

• Allan Savory of the Center for Holistic Management
  in Albuquerque, New Mexico, has redesigned cattle
  ranching to raise the carrying capacity of rangelands,
  which have often been degraded not by overgrazing
  but by undergrazing and grazing the wrong way.
  Savory's solution is to keep the cattle moving from
  place to place, grazing intensively but briefly at each
  site, so that they mimic the dense but constantly moving herds of native grazing animals that coevolved
  with grasslands. Thousands of ranchers are estimated
  to be applying this approach, improving both their
  range and their profits. This "management-intensive
  rotational grazing" method, long standard in New
  Zealand, yields such clearly superior returns that over
  15% of Wisconsin's dairy farms have adopted it in the
  past few years.

• The California Rice Industry Association has discovered that letting nature's diversity flourish can be more
  profitable than forcing it to produce a single product.
  By flooding 150,000 to 200,000 acres of Sacramento
  valley rice fields—about 30% of California's rice-
  growing area—after harvest, farmers are able to create
  seasonal wetlands that support millions of wildfowl,
  replenish groundwater, improve fertility, and yield
  other valuable benefits. In addition, the farmers bale
  and sell the rice straw, whose high silica content—formerly an air-pollution hazard when the straw was
  burned—adds insect resistance and hence value as a
  construction material when it's resold instead.

• John Todd of Living Technologies in Burlington, Ver-
  mont, has used biological Living Machines—linked
  tanks of bacteria, algae, plants, and other organisms—

to turn sewage into clean water. That not only yields cleaner water at a reduced cost, with no toxicity or odor, but it also produces commercially valuable flowers and makes the plant compatible with its residential neighborhood. A similar plant at the Ethel M Chocolates factory in Las Vegas, Nevada, not only handles difficult industrial wastes effectively but is showcased in its public tours.

Although such practices are still evolving, the broad lessons they teach are clear. In almost all climates, soils, and societies, working with nature is more productive than working against it. Reinvesting in nature allows farmers, fishermen, and forest managers to match or exceed the high yields and profits sustained by traditional input-intensive, chemically driven practices. Although much of mainstream business is still headed the other way, the profitability of sustainable, nature-emulating practices is already being proven. In the future, many industries that don't now consider themselves dependent on a biological resource base will become more so as they shift their raw materials and production processes more to biological ones. There is evidence that many business leaders are starting to think this way. The consulting firm Arthur D. Little surveyed a group of North American and European business leaders and found that 83% of them already believe that they can derive "real business value [from implementing a] sustainable-development approach to strategy and operations."

A Broken Compass?

If the road ahead is this clear, why are so many companies straying or falling by the wayside? We believe the reason is that the instruments companies use to set their targets, measure their performance, and hand out rewards are faulty. In other words, the markets are full of distortions and perverse incentives. Of the more than 60 specific forms of misdirection that we have identified,[3] the most obvious involve the ways companies allocate capital and the way governments set policy and impose taxes. Merely correcting these defective practices would uncover huge opportunities for profit.

Consider how companies make purchasing decisions. Decisions to buy small items are typically based on their initial cost rather than their full life-cycle cost, a practice that can add up to major wastage. Distribution transformers that supply electricity to buildings and factories, for example, are a minor item at just $320 apiece, and most companies try to save a quick buck by buying the lowest-price models. Yet nearly all the nation's electricity must flow through transformers, and using the cheaper but less efficient models wastes $1 billion a year. Such examples are legion. Equipping standard new office-lighting circuits with fatter wire that reduces electrical resistance could generate after-tax returns of 193% a year. Instead, wire as thin as the National Electrical Code permits is usually selected because it costs less up-front. But the code is meant only to prevent fires from over-heated wiring, not to save money. Ironically, an electrician who chooses fatter wire—thereby reducing long-term electricity bills—doesn't get the job. After paying for the extra copper, he's no longer the low bidder.

Some companies do consider more than just the initial price in their purchasing decisions but still don't go far enough. Most of them use a crude payback estimate rather than more accurate metrics like discounted cash flow. A few years ago, the median simple payback these

companies were demanding from energy efficiency was
1.9 years. That's equivalent to requiring an after-tax
return of around 71% per year—about six times the
marginal cost of capital.

Most companies also miss major opportunities by
treating their facilities costs as an overhead to be minimized, typically by laying off engineers, rather than as
profit center to be opti-
mized—by using those
engineers to save
resources. Deficient
measurement and
accounting practices
also prevent companies
from allocating costs—

*Many executives think
they already "did" efficiency
in the 1970s, but with
today's far better technologies,
it's profitable
to start over again.*

and waste—with any accuracy. For example, only a few
semiconductor plants worldwide regularly and accurately measure how much energy they're using to produce a unit of chilled water or clean air for their clean-
room production facilities. That makes it hard for them
to improve efficiency. In fact, in an effort to save time,
semiconductor makers frequently build new plants as
exact copies of previous ones—a design method nick-
named "infectious repetitis."

Many executives pay too little attention to saving
resources because they are often a small percentage of
total costs (energy costs run to about 2% in most industries). But those resource savings drop straight to the
bottom line and so represent a far greater percentage of
profits. Many executives also think they already "did"
efficiency in the 1970s, when the oil shock forced them to
rethink old habits. They're forgetting that with today's
far better technologies, it's profitable to start all over
again. Malden Mills, the Massachusetts maker of such

products as Polartec, was already using "efficient" metal-halide lamps in the mid-1990s. But a recent warehouse retrofit reduced the energy used for lighting by another 93%, improved visibility, and paid for itself in 18 months.

The way people are rewarded often creates perverse incentives. Architects and engineers, for example, are traditionally compensated for what they spend, not for what they save. Even the striking economics of the retrofit design for the Chicago office tower described earlier wasn't incentive enough actually to implement it. The property was controlled by a leasing agent who earned a commission every time she leased space, so she didn't want to wait the few extra months needed to refit the building. Her decision to reject the efficiency-quadrupling renovation proved costly for both her and her client. The building was so uncomfortable and expensive to occupy that it didn't lease, so ultimately the owner had to unload it at a fire-sale price. Moreover, the new owner will for the next 20 years be deprived of the opportunity to save capital cost.

In nearly every country on the planet, tax laws penalize jobs and income while subsidizing resource depletion and pollution.

If corporate practices obscure the benefits of natural capitalism, government policy positively undermines it. In nearly every country on the planet, tax laws penalize what we want more of—jobs and income—while subsidizing what we want less of—resource depletion and pollution. In every state but Oregon, regulated utilities are rewarded for selling more energy, water, and other resources, and penalized for selling less, even if increased production would cost more than improved customer efficiency. In most of America's arid western states, use-it-or-lose-it water laws encourage inefficient water consumption. Additionally, in many towns, inefficient use of land is enforced through outdated regulations, such as guidelines for ultrawide suburban streets recommended by 1950s civil-defense planners to accommodate the heavy equipment needed to clear up rubble after a nuclear attack.

The costs of these perverse incentives are staggering: $300 billion in annual energy wasted in the United States, and $1 trillion already misallocated to unnecessary air-conditioning equipment and the power supplies to run it (about 40% of the nation's peak electric load). Across the entire economy, unneeded expenditures to subsidize, encourage, and try to remedy inefficiency and damage that should not have occurred in the first place probably account for most, if not all, of the GDP growth of the past two decades. Indeed, according to former World Bank economist Herman Daly and his colleague John Cobb (along with many other analysts), Americans are hardly better off than they were in 1980. But if the U.S. government and private industry could redirect the dollars currently earmarked for remedial costs toward reinvestment in natural and human capital, they could bring about a genuine improvement in the nation's welfare. Companies, too, are finding that wasting resources also means wasting money and people. These intertwined forms of waste have equally intertwined solutions. Firing the unproductive tons, gallons, and kilowatt-hours often makes it possible to keep the people, who will have more and better work to do.

Recognizing the Scarcity Shift

In the end, the real trouble with our economic compass is that it points in exactly the wrong direction. Most businesses are behaving as if people were still scarce and nature still abundant—the conditions that helped to fuel the first Industrial Revolution. At that time, people were relatively scarce compared with the present-day population. The rapid mechanization of the textile industries caused explosive economic growth that created labor shortages in the factory and the field. The Industrial Revolution, responding to those shortages and mechanizing one industry after another, made people a hundred times more productive than they had ever been.

The logic of economizing on the scarcest resource, because it limits progress, remains correct. But the pattern of scarcity is shifting: now people aren't scarce but nature is. This shows up first in industries that depend directly on ecological health. Here, production is increasingly constrained by fish rather than by boats and nets, by forests rather than by chain saws, by fertile topsoil rather than by plows. Moreover, unlike the traditional factors of industrial production—capital and labor—the biological limiting factors cannot be substituted for one other. In the industrial system, we can easily exchange machinery for labor. But no technology or amount of money can substitute for a stable climate and a productive biosphere. Even proper pricing can't replace the priceless.

Natural capitalism addresses those problems by reintegrating ecological with economic goals. Because it is both necessary and profitable, it will subsume traditional industrialism within a new economy and a new paradigm of production, just as industrialism previously subsumed agrarianism. The companies that first make the changes we have described will have a competitive edge. Those that don't make that effort won't be a problem because ultimately they won't be around. In making that choice, as Henry Ford said, "Whether you believe you can, or whether you believe you can't, you're absolutely right."

Notes

1. Our book, *Natural Capitalism,* provides hundreds of examples of how companies of almost every type and size, often through modest shifts in business logic and practice, have dramatically improved their bottom lines.

2. Nonproprietary details are posted at http://www.hypercar.com.

3. Summarized in the report "Climate: Making Sense *and* Making Money" at http://www.rmi.org/catalog/climate.htm.

Originally published in May–June 1999
Reprint 99309

Bringing the Environment Down to Earth

FOREST L. REINHARDT

Executive Summary

THE DEBATE ON BUSINESS and the environment has typically been framed in simple yes-or-no terms: "Does it pay to be green?" But the environment, like other business issues, requires a more complex approach—one that demands more than such all-or-nothing thinking. Managers need to ask instead, "Under what circumstances do particular kinds of environmental investments deliver returns to shareholders?"

This article presents five approaches that managers can take to identify those circumstances and integrate the environment into their business thinking. These approaches will enable companies with the right industry structure, competitive position, and managerial skills to reconcile their responsibility to shareholders with the pressure to be faithful stewards of the earth's resources.

35

Some companies can distance themselves from competitors by differentiating their products and commanding higher prices for them. Others may be able to "manage" their competitors by imposing a set of private regulations or by helping to shape the rules written by government officials. Still others may be able to cut costs and help the environment simultaneously. Almost all can learn to improve their management of risk and thus reduce the outlays associated with accidents, lawsuits, and boycotts. And some companies may even be able to make systemic changes that will redefine competition in their markets.

All five approaches can help managers bring the environment down to earth. And that means bringing the environment back into the fold of business problems and determining when it *really* pays to be green.

T HE DEBATE ON BUSINESS and the environment has been framed in simplistic yes-or-no terms: "Does it pay to be green?" Many business school academics and environmental leaders have answered yes. Yet businesspeople are skeptical—and rightly so, since they instinctively reject such all-or-nothing thinking in other contexts: Does it pay to build your next plant in Singapore? To increase your debt-to-equity ratio? To sue your competitors for patent infringement? The answer, of course, is "It depends." And so it is with environmental questions: the right policy depends on the circumstances confronting the company and the strategy it has chosen.

Much of the writing about business and the environment ignores that basic point. (See "Beware of What You

Know" at the end of this article.) The underlying assumption is that the earth is sick—and that therefore it *ought* to be profitable to find ways to help it return to good health. Promoting such causes and activities as

Managers need to go beyond the question "Does it pay to be green?"

recycling, solar energy, and small-scale agriculture should redound to business's benefit. But this is faulty reasoning. The truth is, environmental problems do not automatically create opportunities to make money. At the same time, the opposite stance—that it never pays for a company to invest in improving its environmental performance—is also incorrect.

That's why managers should look at environmental problems as business issues. They should make environmental investments for the same reasons they make other investments: because they expect them to deliver positive returns or to reduce risks. Managers need to go beyond the question "Does it pay to be green?" and ask instead "Under what circumstances do particular kinds of environmental investments deliver benefits to shareholders?"

I have identified five approaches that companies can take to integrate the environment into their business thinking. Some companies can distance themselves from their competitors by differentiating products and commanding higher prices for them. Others may be able to "manage" their competitors by imposing a set of private regulations or by helping to shape the rules written by government officials. Still others may be able to cut costs and help the environment simultaneously. Almost all of them can learn to improve their management of risk and thus reduce the outlays associated with accidents, lawsuits, and boycotts. And some companies may even be able to make systemic changes that will redefine competition in their markets.

The appeal of any of the five approaches will depend on the time horizon over which they are evaluated. As with other business problems, the environmental strategy that maximizes short-term cash flow is probably not the one that positions the company optimally for the long run. That's true of all business strategies in general, of course, but it especially applies to the environmental arena because benefits from environmental investments are often realized over long periods.

All of the approaches can help managers to bring the environment down to earth: to think systematically and realistically about the application of traditional business principles to environmental problems. They can enable some companies—those with the right industry structure, competitive position, and managerial skills—to deliver increased value to shareholders while making improvements in their environmental performance.

Differentiating Products

The idea behind environmental product differentiation is straightforward: companies create products or employ processes that offer greater environmental benefits or impose smaller environmental costs than those of their competitors. Such efforts may raise the business's costs, but they may also enable it to command higher prices, to capture additional market share, or both.

Consider an example from the textile industry. When textile manufacturers dye cotton or rayon fabric, they immerse the material in a bath containing dyes dissolved in water and then add salt to push the dyes out of the solution and into the cloth. Ciba Specialty

Chemicals, a Swiss manufacturer of textile dyes, has introduced dyes that fix more readily to the fabric and therefore require less salt.

The new dyes help Ciba's customers in three ways. First, they lower the outlays for salt: textile companies using Ciba's new dyes can reduce their costs for salt by up to 2% of revenues—a significant drop in an industry with razor-thin profit margins. Second, they reduce manufacturers' costs for water treatment. Used bathwater—full of salt and unfixed dye—must be treated before it is released into rivers or streams (even in low-income countries where environmental standards may be relatively lax). Less salt and less unfixed dye mean lower water-treatment costs. Third, the new dyes' higher fixation rates make quality control easier, thus lowering the costs of rework.

Ciba's dyes are the result of years of development in the laboratory. They are protected against imitation by patents and by the unpatentable but complicated chemistry that goes into making them. For those reasons, Ciba can charge more for its dyes and capture some of the value it is creating for customers.

If this sounds like any other story about industrial marketing—add value to your customers' activities and then capture some of that value yourself—it should. Lowering a customer's environmental costs adds value to its operations just as surely as a new machine that enhances labor productivity does.

Three conditions are required for success with environmental product differentiation, and Ciba's approach satisfies all three. First, the company has identified customers who are willing to pay more for an environmentally friendly product. Second, it has been able to communicate its product's environmental benefits credibly.

And third, it has been able to protect itself from imitators for long enough to profit on its investment.

If any of those three conditions break down, the product differentiation approach will not work. StarKist, the canned tuna subsidiary of H.J. Heinz, made this discovery when it decided to market dolphin-safe tuna.

Over the years, traditional techniques for catching tuna have caused the death of millions of dolphins. That's because the yellowfin tuna of the eastern tropical Pacific—the staple of tuna canners—often swim underneath schools of dolphin. A boat's crew would locate and chase a school of dolphins, drop a basketlike net under the school when the chase was over, and then haul in the tuna and the dolphins, often killing the dolphins in the process. Criticism of this practice, dating from the 1970s, intensified dramatically in 1989, when an environmental activist group released gruesome video footage of dolphins dying in the course of tuna-fishing operations.

In April 1990, StarKist announced that it would sell only tuna from the western Pacific, where tuna do not swim beneath dolphins. But the company ran into problems with all three conditions for success.

First, contrary to the company's survey findings that people would pay significantly more for dolphin-safe tuna, consumers proved unwilling to pay a premium for a cheap source of protein. It didn't help that western Pacific tuna was not yellowfin but skipjack, which people found inferior in taste.

Second, although StarKist made known its efforts to protect dolphins, it turned out that the fishing techniques practiced in the western Pacific were no environmental bargain. For each dolphin saved in the eastern Pacific, thousands of immature tuna and dozens of sharks, turtles, and other marine animals died in the western part of the ocean.

Finally, the company had no protection from imitators. Its main competitors, Bumble Bee and Chicken of the Sea, matched StarKist's move almost at once.

It would be easy to take from this story a universally gloomy message about the prospects for environmental product differentiation in consumer markets. Environmental quality, after all, is a public good: everyone gets to enjoy it regardless of who pays for it. From the standpoint of economic self-interest, one might wonder why any individual would be willing to pay for a public good.

But that view is too narrow. People willingly pay for public goods all the time: sometimes in cash, when they contribute to charities, and often in time, when they give blood, clean up litter from parks and highways, or rinse their soda bottles for recycling. The trick for companies is to find the right public good—or to offer an imaginative bundle of public and private goods—that will appeal to a targeted market.

For example, sellers of "designer beef "—meat from cattle that have not been exposed to herbicides or hormones—offer consumers potential health benefits (a private good) in addition to a more environmentally friendly product (a public good). And Patagonia, a California maker of recreational clothing, has developed a loyal base of high-income customers partly

A company can still come out ahead if it forces competitors to raise their costs even more.

because its brand identity includes a commitment to conservation. Patagonia and the beef marketers have not only cleared the willingness-to-pay hurdle but have also found ways to communicate credibly about their products and to protect themselves from imitators through branding.

Managing Your Competitors

Not all companies will be able to increase their profits through environmental product differentiation. But some may be able to derive environmental and business benefits by working to change the rules of the game so that the playing field tilts in their favor. A company may need to incur higher costs to respond to environmental pressure, but it can still come out ahead if it forces competitors to raise their costs even more.

How can that be done? By joining with similarly positioned companies within an industry to set private standards, or by convincing government to create regulations that favor your product.

The first approach has been particularly successful in the chemical industry. In 1984, after toxic gas escaped from the plant of a Union Carbide subsidiary in Bhopal, India, and killed more than 2,000 people, the industry's image was tarnished, and it faced the threat of punitive government regulation. The industry recognized that it had to act—to forestall government regulations and improve its safety record without incurring unreasonable costs. As a result, the leading companies in the Chemical Manufacturers Association created an initiative called Responsible Care and developed a set of private regulations that the association's members adopted in 1988.

The U.S. companies that make up the CMA must comply with six management codes that cover such areas as pollution prevention, process safety, and emergency response. If they cannot show good-faith efforts to comply, their membership will be terminated. The initiative has enhanced the association's environmental reputation by producing results. Between 1988 and 1994, for example, U.S. chemical companies reduced their environmental releases of toxic materials by almost 50%. Although other industries were also achieving significant reductions during this period, the chemical industry's reductions were steeper than the national average.

Moreover, the big companies that organized Responsible Care have improved their competitive positions. They spend a lower percentage of their revenues to improve their safety record than smaller competitors in the CMA; similarly, they spend a lower percentage of revenues on the monitoring, reporting, and administrative costs of the regulations. Finally, because the association's big companies do a great deal of business abroad, they have been able to persuade the CMA's foreign counterparts to initiate their own private regulatory programs— even in developing countries where one might expect little enthusiasm for tough environmental policies.

The prerequisites for the success of private regulatory programs like Responsible Care are the same as those for government regulatory programs. The regulators must be able to set measurable performance standards, have access to information to verify compliance, and be in a position to enforce their rules. Private programs also need at least the tacit

Companies that want to tie their competitors' hands can work with government regulators.

approval of government: if they are incompatible with other rules such as antitrust laws, the private regulations won't hold up. And private regulations must cover all relevant competitors: it is no use for some companies to tie the hands of others if a third group has the potential to undercut them both.

The commodity chemicals business is better suited than most to private regulatory initiatives. Performance standards are comparatively easy to define because, for example, a perchloroethylene plant in Louisiana looks a lot like a perchloroethylene plant in New Jersey or Italy. Verifying compliance is not a problem either, because the companies constantly sell products to one another and thus can examine competitors' plants. Companies that violate the rules can be ousted from the association—even though it is illegal under antitrust law for the CMA to make compliance with Responsible Care a prerequisite for doing business with association members.

As an alternative to private regulation, companies that want to tie their competitors' hands can work with government regulators. Gasoline marketers in California followed this strategy when they helped design new state rules mandating reformulated gasoline to reduce air pollution.

Despite aggressive regulation in California in the 1970s and 1980s, many urban areas in the late 1980s were still not close to meeting national standards for smog, and regulators were threatening to require the use of methanol or ethanol fuels, or even to phase out gasoline-powered cars altogether. Rather than watch their markets erode, California gasoline refiners introduced reformulated gasolines containing a compound called methyl tertiary butyl ether (MTBE), and then gained regulatory mandates effectively requiring the use of these fuels.

The California gasoline refiners were in a strong position to use environmental regulation for strategic purposes. First, regulators were more than willing to act, given the state's ongoing smog problems. Second, the costs of the regulations would be spread among all of California's automobile drivers, so the chance of organized opposition was slight. Third, competitors from other states would have an even more difficult time selling in the California market. Outsiders already faced steep barriers to entry: pipeline capacity to California was limited, and the costs of transporting gasoline from, say, Texas were high. California's rules for reformulated gasoline erected another barrier and increased the collective pricing power of the California refiners.

Although the overall strategy was sound, the reformulated-gasoline policies have not been as effective as hoped. MTBE reduces air pollution, but leaks of the chemical have polluted groundwater. MTBE was found in municipal drinking-water wells in Santa Monica in 1997; it subsequently appeared in groundwater supplies elsewhere in the state. As a result, continued regulatory approval for MTBE use is now in jeopardy. Using environmental regulation strategically, as this example demonstrates, has both benefits and risks.

The approach of forcing rivals to match one's own behavior is fundamentally different from that of environmental product differentiation. A manager thinking about the choice between the two approaches needs to ask, Am I better off if my competitors match my investment or if they don't? If a company's customers are willing to reward it for improved environmental performance, the company will want to forestall imitation by competitors. But if its customers cannot be induced to pay a premium for an environmentally preferable good, then it may want its competitors to have to match its behavior.

Saving Costs

A third approach to reconciling shareholder value with environmental management focuses not on competitors but on internal cost reductions. Some organizations are able to cut costs and improve environmental performance simultaneously.

For instance, as many travelers know, major hotel chains over the past decade have tried to follow this approach. These companies' tactics include reducing their solid-waste generation and cutting their water and energy use. Many hotels have replaced small bottles of shampoo and lotion with bulk dispensers, saving money and reducing waste. One company saved nearly $37,000 per year after installing dispensers at a cost of $91,000. Others use recycled packaging for amenities. Inter-Continental Hotels, for instance, reportedly saves $300,000 per year in this way at its ten properties in the United States and Canada.

Industrial companies have cut costs and enhanced environmental performance at the same time by redesigning inflexible or wasteful routines. Consider Xerox's efforts. After nearly three decades of market dominance, the company found its traditional markets crowded in the late 1980s with well-funded new entrants. Xerox's market share declined, and its margins eroded precipitously.

In 1990, the company's executives responded with a new management initiative—the Environmental Leadership Program—that eventually included waste reduction efforts, product "take-back" schemes, and design-for-environment initiatives. By the mid-1990s, Xerox's large manufacturing complex in Webster, New York, was sending only 2% of its hazardous waste to landfills. In the early 1990s, even before the program had a chance to bear much fruit, Xerox's executives were already labeling the program an unqualified success.

Xerox's story illustrates a common pattern: dramatic cost savings are often found when a company is under tremendous pressure. As long as Xerox was the unchallenged market leader, it could afford to be easygoing about cost savings—and it was. Yet when things got rough, it rose to the occasion with creative initiatives.

Observers of this pattern have wondered whether stringent environmental regulation could put the same kind of pressure on companies that competitive pressure does. They argue that "free" opportunities to improve environmental performance—in which the direct benefits to the company exceed the costs—are ubiquitous and that stricter regulatory requirements or changes in the tax code could force companies to uncover them. (For an example of such an argument, see Chapter 1, "A Road Map for Natural Capitalism.")

Environmental investments are worthwhile only if they deliver value after all the management costs have been included.

Others disagree. They point out that managers are paid to minimize costs and wonder how adding new regulatory constraints could possibly reduce costs. Economists call this dispute the "free lunch" debate. The underlying issue is the appropriate level of government regulation.

The free lunch advocates overstate their case. Even low-hanging fruit can only be gathered after an investment of management time, and that resource is hardly free. Investments in environmental improvement, like all other investments, are worthwhile only if they deliver value after all the management costs have been included.

Fortunately, though, companies can remain agnostic on the question of whether free opportunities to improve environmental performance are widespread. From a business point of view, even if such opportunities are rare, managers should look for them as long as the search doesn't cost much in terms of their time or other resources.

Managing Environmental Risk

For many businesspeople, environmental management means risk management. Their primary objective is to avoid the costs that are associated with an industrial accident, a consumer boycott, or an environmental lawsuit. Fortunately, effective management of the business risk stemming from environmental problems can itself be a source of competitive advantage.

Alberta-Pacific Forest Industries, a Canadian venture of Japanese companies, has discovered that the voluntary provision of environmental goods can cost-effectively reduce long-term business risk. In 1993, the Japanese companies and their Canadian partners negotiated timber-harvesting rights on a vast tract of government-owned aspen and spruce forests in northern Alberta. The venture planned to build a conventional pulp mill that would use chlorine bleaching. It also planned to run the forests as they had always been run in western Canada, where, as one forestry manager put it, "There was never a plan for forest management, and 'forest planning' just meant 'fiber extraction.'"

Effective management of environmental risk can itself be a source of competitive advantage.

But the project ran into a buzz saw of opposition from local farmers, aboriginal residents of northern Alberta, and environmental activists from around the world. Alberta-Pacific went back to the drawing board. It returned with plans for a mill that would keep pollution levels far lower than the government required; it also developed forest management policies that would substantially reduce traditional clear-cutting. In addition, it promised to hold regular public meetings, to communicate explicitly about the environmental impact of the company's operations, to carry out collaborative research with biologists from outside the company, and to provide recreational access to the woods.

The costs of these changes were modest and, in return, Alberta-Pacific improved its community relations and achieved more stable long-term costs. The changes are an insurance policy against regulatory difficulties, sour community relations, business interruptions, and related cost shocks. The leaders of Alberta-Pacific have realized that their ability to operate is contingent on society's approval, that the formal property rights they possess are necessary but not sufficient for them to cut timber and run mills, and that environmental improvements can make sense as risk management devices.

If Alberta-Pacific had not heeded the concerns of local residents and environmentalists, it likely would have been prohibited from using the land at all. And the stakes were high—the costs of raw materials were on a level one might find in Indonesia or Brazil, but the political and exchange-rate risks were far lower. The venture's small initial investments in the environment allowed it to profit from use of the forest.

Indeed, any company can benefit from an audit of its environmental insurance policies and risk management systems. Is the company buying the right policies? Is it retaining risk when the coverage is overpriced? Is it rewarding managers who reduce risk in their own operations or subsidizing risky behavior by failing to police it adequately?

Managers at Chevron are trying to answer those questions. They're analyzing the relative value of investing more in sprinkler systems, rapid response teams, maintenance, and other systems and activities that reduce environmental risk. They are also working to change employees' attitudes toward environmental and safety issues in order to reduce the risk of accidents. Chevron has found that environmental risk can be managed more effectively both by applying more rigorous quantitative analysis and by increasing its emphasis on training and cultural change programs.

It is not easy to prove that investments in environmental risk management are bearing fruit. And the potential for overinvestment is a concern. But just as it is for more traditional business risks, some investment in environmental risk management is prudent. (For a comparison of environmental and traditional risk management, see "Integrating Risk Management" at the end of this article.")

Redefining Markets

Some companies are following several approaches at once. In the process, they are rewriting the competitive rules in their markets.

As we've seen, Xerox has been a leader in searching for cost reductions. More dramatically, it has also attempted to redefine its business model. Rather than simply selling office equipment, it retains responsibility for the equipment's disposal, and it takes back products from customers when they are superseded by new technology. The machines are then disassembled, remanufactured to incorporate new technology, and resold at the same price as new machines. This practice enables Xerox to reduce its overall costs and also to make life difficult for competitors who lack similar capabilities. Customers benefit, too, because they no longer have to worry about the disposal of cumbersome machinery.

Rethinking traditional notions about property rights, as Xerox has done, is a useful way of discovering corporate opportunities to redefine markets based on environmental challenges. Instead of transferring all rights and responsibilities of ownership to their customers, Xerox and other manufacturers are retaining the obligation of disposal in return for control of the product at the end of its useful life.

Because of that initiative, Xerox reportedly saved $50 million in 1990, its first year. A drop in raw-materials purchases was the most significant component of the cost savings—fewer natural resources were used to make new machines. By 1995, Xerox estimated that it was saving more than several hundred million dollars annually by taking back used machines. Other manufacturers of electronic equipment such as Kodak, IBM, Canon, and Hewlett-Packard have undertaken similar initiatives.

Companies like Xerox that combine innovations in property rights and advances in technology may be able to create very strong competitive positions. Monsanto, DuPont, Novartis, and others are using this approach to redefine the agriculture industry. Instead of making traditional insecticides for crop pests, the companies transfer genetic material from naturally occurring bacteria to seeds so that the plants themselves become inedible to insects. These new seeds are highly profitable; they avoid the financial and environmental costs of making, transporting, and applying insecticides. But the path has not been free of rocks: environmental groups and consumers, especially in Europe, have protested the sale of genetically engineered products in their markets.

Like Xerox, Monsanto also redefined the property rights that go with its product. In order to recover its investment in seed technology, Monsanto needs repeat customers every year. But farmers commonly engage in a practice known as "brown bagging"—they save seeds left over from one year's crop to plant the following year. In return for the right to use the new type of seeds, Monsanto requires farmers to stop brown bagging and to submit to inspections to ensure compliance.

The ambitious strategies that Monsanto and Xerox are following have attracted a great deal of attention. But such strategies can entail significant market, regulatory, and scientific risks; they're not for every company—or even for every industry. The companies that appear to be succeeding are leaders in industries that face intensifying environmental pressure. Those companies have the research capabilities to develop new ways of delivering valuable services to their customers, the staying power to impose their vision of the future on their markets, and the resources to manage the inevitable risks. Moreover, by creating an appealing vision of a more profitable and environmentally responsible future, they may be better able to attract and retain the managers, scientists, and engineers who will enable them to build on their initial success.

Beyond All-or-Nothing

All-or-nothing arguments have dominated thinking about business and the environment. But it doesn't have to be that way. Consider how ideas about product quality have changed. At first, conventional wisdom held that improvements in quality had to be purchased at a cost of extra dollars and management attention. Then assertions were made that "quality is free": new savings would always pay for investments in improved quality. Now companies have arrived at a more nuanced view. They recognize that improving quality can sometimes lead to cost reductions, but they acknowledge that the right strategy depends on the company and its customers' requirements. It is time for business thinking on the environment to reach a similar middle ground.

As we've seen, environmental problems are best analyzed as business problems. Whether companies are attempting to differentiate their products, tie their competitors' hands, reduce internal costs, manage risk, or even reinvent their industry, the basic tasks do not change when the word "environmental" is included in the proposition.

Does all this mean that questions of social responsibility can be safely ignored? Not at all—but they're only one part of the equation. Companies aren't in business to solve the world's problems, nor should they be. After all, they have shareholders who want to see a return on their investments. That's why managers need to bring the environment back into the fold of business problems and determine when it *really* pays to be green.

Not all companies can profit from concern about the environment. Others will be able to do so by following one—and in some cases more than one—of the approaches described here. At any rate, a systematic look at environmental management opportunities is worth the time. Imaginative and capable managers who look at the environment as a business issue will find that the universe of possibilities is greater than they ever realized.

Beware of What You Know

TREATING ENVIRONMENTAL ISSUES as business problems sounds straightforward, but it's not easy. The following assumptions, all of which are common in business thinking, make it difficult to reframe the issues.

Environmental problems are, first and foremost, matters of social responsibility. While considerations of social responsibility are important, executives who frame environmental problems solely in those terms may overlook the business opportunities and risks that come with such problems. Treating environmental issues like other business issues can lead to more creative problem solving as well as better bottom-line results.

Environmental questions are cause for pessimism. In most arenas, successful managers search for opportunity in adversity and find in complex problems a chance to separate their companies from competitors. So it's striking to hear how passive and pessimistic they sound when talking about environmental issues. They take that approach because they associate it not just with extra costs but also with a loss of control over their own operations. But, as the examples in this article show, it doesn't have to be that way.

Environmental management is a zero-sum game. For every winner in a zero-sum contest, there is a loser. Thus if the environment wins, the company loses, and vice versa. That view is prevalent in part because it fits with the widespread perception that environmental problems are political or moral issues. Elections and crusades are win-lose by definition and by design, but businesses don't ordinarily operate that way. Instead, they look for chances to benefit themselves and others simultaneously. Some environmental problems are inevitably win-lose, but it's a mistake to think that none of them can be recast.

Government and environmental groups are the company's adversaries. At times, that view is justified; some regulators and advocates are indeed hostile to business. But government and nonprofit organizations will always play a role in environmental management—the only question is what kind of role. Sometimes it makes sense to circle the wagons against an external threat. But sometimes it makes sense for a company to ally itself with regulators or advocates against the competitors.

While managers must remain on guard against undue pessimism and passivity in dealing with environmental problems, they also need to beware of wishful or insular thinking that can intensify their environmental problems and cost their shareholders unnecessary money. These are some of the common pitfalls:

- **Letting business interests sway your opinion of scientific and economic analysis.** Managers shouldn't let the costs of solving an environmental problem affect their judgment of the scientific evidence that identifies the problem. Pulling the wool over your own eyes may convince you that you've averted disaster. In the long run, however, the fact that you can't see it doesn't mean you're hidden from danger.

- **Assuming that maintaining the status quo is an option.** It is common to use the status quo as a baseline—to look at the way things are today and to think about how you can change things on your own. But some change is likely to occur in any case, and managers need to be realistic about their ability to keep things as they are.

- **Avoiding dissenting opinion.** People find it comfortable to talk with those who share their views. Managers need to keep their minds open to the new perspectives and new facts that can come from regular conversations with government officials, environmentalists, and others outside their usual circle.

Those problems can all be overcome. If executives bring to environmental decision making the same kind of optimism, opportunism, analytic thinking, and openness that they instinctively bring to bear on other business problems, both their companies and the environment will benefit.

Integrating Risk Management

THINKING ABOUT ENVIRONMENTAL improvement as a risk management strategy, as managers at Alberta-Pacific and Chevron do, leads to the question, Should companies try to manage environmental risk in the same ways they manage other business risks?

In many companies, environmental risk is handled by the department that deals with environmental, health, and safety issues, while the management of currency and other financial risk is centralized under the treasurer or the financial officers. Those different parts of the organization usually take widely varying approaches to risk management and may even be ignorant of each other's activities.

There are legitimate reasons for managing environmental risk differently from other risks. Environmental risk is exceedingly difficult to assess quantitatively: no one can really know the probability of an accident occurring at a particular factory. By contrast, it's easier, say, to assess the probability that the dollar will move up or down against the yen—and market instruments exist that allow companies to hedge against such a risk.

Although it makes sense to manage environmental risk differently from other business risks, companies commonly make a serious mistake in the process: they rely too heavily on command-and-control mechanisms—in the form of procedural manuals and rules—to govern line managers' behavior. That approach impedes flexibility and fails to tap the expertise of individual line managers—the same problems that arise when government imposes command-and-control regulations.

Some reliance on command-and-control policies is probably necessary, but there are other ways to ensure effective risk management, and the wise risk manager uses a variety of approaches. A manager's environmental performance can be made a factor in determining incentive pay. Similarly, it can be considered in regular performance reviews and in the promotion process. And as information about environmental risks and their effects on a company's financials improves, it will become increasingly possible to handle environmental risk like other risks within the organization. For example, companies often buy insurance against environmental liability at the corporate level but don't charge operating managers for their unit's portion of the premiums. If they did, the managers' incentives would be better aligned with those of the company.

But even the steps outlined here will not change the inherently muddy nature of investments in environmental risk management. You can never be sure, even long after the fact, that investments designed to prevent an accident or a lawsuit were the right ones. That's why even sensible investments in risk management are extremely vulnerable to cost-cutting pressure. At the same time, the inability to determine measurable results can lead to overspending on risk reduction as well as to empire building in the environmental office.

To avoid such problems, senior managers need to ensure that those responsible for environmental risk are clear about the potential benefits of their investments. Managers whose responsibilities include environmental risk should be pushed to articulate why the level and type of investments they have chosen are appropriate. Furthermore, they need to communicate with those responsible for other sorts of business risk so that the approaches are consistent. That doesn't mean the approaches should be identical. Until managers have the same information about environmental risk as they have about currency risk, it won't make sense to manage the two in the same way—and that day is a long way off. But environmental risk management should not be shoved off to one side of the organizational chart and managed as a special case. Integrating it into the company's overall risk management approaches will yield better decisions over the long run.

Originally published in July–August 1999
Reprint 99408

Growth Through Global Sustainability

An Interview with Monsanto's CEO, Robert B. Shapiro

JOAN MAGRETTA

Executive Summary

ROBERT SHAPIRO ASKS a tough question: How do we face the prospect that creating a profitable, growing company might require intolerable abuse of the natural world? Monsanto—with its history in the chemicals indus-try—is an unlikely candidate to be creating cutting-edge environmental solutions, but that is precisely what it is doing. The need for sustainability is transforming the com-pany's thinking about growth.

Changes in global environmental conditions will soon create an unprecedented economic discontinuity. To invent new businesses around the concept of environ-mental sustainability, Shapiro begins with a simple law of physics: A closed system like the earth's cannot support an unlimited increase of material things. It can, however, withstand exponential growth in information. So

Monsanto is exploring ways to substitute information for "stuff" and services for products.

In its agricultural business, the company is genetically coding plants to repel or destroy harmful insects. Putting the right information in the plant makes pesticides unnecessary. Information replaces stuff; productivity increases and waste is reduced. Monsanto also is looking at its carpet business. Today it costs too much to reuse carpets. But Monsanto realized that if the manufacturer owned the carpet and merely leased it to customers, it might be feasible to put in more cost up front and make the carpet more recyclable. Monsanto is reexamining the total life cycle of all its products and asking, What do people really need to buy? Do they need stuff or do they need a service? And what would be the economics of providing that service?

Robert B. Shapiro, chairman and CEO of Monsanto Company, based in St. Louis, Missouri, sees the conundrum facing his company this way. On the one hand, if a business doesn't grow, it will die. And the world economy must grow to keep pace with the needs of population growth. On the other hand, how does a company face the prospect that growing and being profitable could require intolerable abuse of the natural world? In Shapiro's words, "It's the kind of question that people who choose to spend their lives working in business can't shrug off or avoid easily. And it has important implications for business strategy."

Sustainable development is the term for the dual imperative—economic growth and environmental sustainability—that has been gaining ground among business leaders since the 1992 United Nations Earth Summit in

Rio de Janeiro. As Shapiro puts it, "We can't expect the rest of the world to abandon their economic aspirations just so we can continue to enjoy clean air and water. That is neither ethically correct nor likely to be permitted by the billions of people in the developing world who expect the quality of their lives to improve."

Monsanto—with its history in the chemicals industry—may seem an unlikely company to lead the way on an emerging environmental issue. But a number of resource- and energy-intensive companies criticized as environmental offenders in the 1980s have been the first to grasp the strategic implications of sustainability.

Monsanto, in fact, is seeking growth through sustainability, betting on a strategic discontinuity from which few businesses will be immune. To borrow Stuart L. Hart's phrase, Monsanto is moving "beyond greening." (See Chapter 5, "Beyond Greening: Strategies for a Sustainable World.") In the following interview with HBR editor-at-large Joan Magretta, the 58-year-old Shapiro discusses how Monsanto has moved from a decade of progress in pollution prevention and clean-up to spotting opportunities for revenue growth in environmentally sustainable new products and technologies.

HBR: Why is sustainability becoming an important component of your strategic thinking?

Robert B. Shapiro: Today there are about 5.8 billion people in the world. About 1.5 billion of them live in conditions of abject poverty—a subsistence life that simply can't be romanticized as some form of simpler, preindustrial lifestyle. These people spend their days trying to get food and firewood so that they can make it to the next day. As many as 800 million people are so severely malnourished that they can neither work nor participate in family life. That's where we are today. And, as far as I know, no demographer questions that the world population will just about double by sometime around 2030.

Without radical change, the kind of world implied by those numbers is unthinkable. It's a world of mass migrations and environmental degradation on an unimaginable scale. At best, it means the preservation of a few islands of privilege and prosperity in a sea of misery and violence.

Our nation's economic system evolved in an era of cheap energy and careless waste disposal, when limits seemed irrelevant. None of us today, whether we're managing a house or running a business, is living in a sustainable way. It's not a question of good guys and bad guys. There is no point in saying, If only those bad guys would go out of business, then the world would be fine. The whole system has to change; there's a huge opportunity for reinvention.

We're entering a time of perhaps unprecedented discontinuity. Businesses grounded in the old model will become obsolete and die. At Monsanto, we're trying to invent some new businesses around the concept of environmental sustainability. We may not yet know exactly what those businesses will look like, but we're willing to place some bets because the world cannot avoid needing sustainability in the long run.

Can you explain how what you're describing is a discontinuity?

Years ago, we would approach strategic planning by considering "the environment"—that is, the economic, technological, and competitive context of the business—and we'd forecast how it would change over the planning horizon. Forecasting usually meant extrapolating recent trends. So we almost never predicted the critical discontinuities in which the real money was made and lost— the changes that really determined the future of the business. Niels Bohr was right when he said it is difficult to make predictions—especially about the future. But every consumer marketer knows that you can rely on demographics. Many market discontinuities were predictable—and future ones can still be predicted—based on observable, incontrovertible facts such as baby booms and busts, life expectancies, and immigration patterns. Sustainable development is one of those discontinuities. Far from being a soft issue grounded in emotion or ethics, sustainable development involves cold, rational business logic.

This discontinuity is occurring because we are encountering physical limits. You can see it coming arithmetically. Sustainability involves the laws of nature—physics, chemistry, and biology—and the recognition that the world is a closed system. What we thought was boundless has limits, and we're beginning to hit them. That's going to change a lot of today's fundamental economics, it's going to change prices, and it's going to change what's socially acceptable.

Is sustainability an immediate issue today in any of Monsanto's businesses?

In some businesses, it's probably less apparent why sustainability is so critical. But in our agricultural business, we can't avoid it. In the twentieth century, we have been able to feed people by bringing more acreage into production and by increasing productivity through fertilizers, pesticides, and irrigation. But current agricultural practice isn't sustainable: we've lost something on the order of 15% of our topsoil over the last 20 years or so, irrigation is increasing the salinity of soil, and the petrochemicals we rely on aren't renewable.

Most arable land is already under cultivation. Attempts to open new farmland are causing severe ecological damage. So in the best case, we have the same amount of land to work with and twice as many people to feed. It comes down to resource productivity. You have to get twice the yield from every acre of land just to maintain current levels of poverty and malnutrition.

Now, even if you wanted to do it in an unsustainable way, no technology today would let you double productivity. With current best practices applied to all the acreage in the world, you'd get about a third of the way toward feeding the whole population. The conclusion is that new technology is the only alternative to one of two disasters: not feeding people—letting the Malthusian process work its magic on the population—or ecological catastrophe.

What new technology are you talking about?

We don't have 100 years to figure that out; at best, we have decades. In that time frame, I know of only two viable candidates: biotechnology and information technology. I'm treating them as though they're separate, but biotechnology is really a subset of information technology because it is about DNA-encoded information.

Using information is one of the ways to increase productivity without abusing nature. A closed system like the earth's can't withstand a systematic increase of material things, but it can support exponential increases of information and knowledge. If economic development means using more stuff, then those who argue that growth and environmental sustainability are incompatible are right. And if we grow by using more stuff, I'm afraid we'd better start looking for a new planet.

But sustainability and development might be compatible if you could create value and satisfy people's needs by increasing the information component of what's produced and diminishing the amount of stuff.

How does biotechnology replace stuff with information in agriculture?

We can genetically code a plant, for example, to repel or destroy harmful insects. That means we don't have to spray the plant with pesticides—with stuff. Up to 90% of what's sprayed on crops today is wasted. Most of it ends up on the soil. If we put the right information in the plant, we waste less stuff and increase productivity. With biotechnology, we can accomplish that. It's not that chemicals are inherently bad. But they are less efficient than biology because you have to manufacture and distribute and apply them.

If companies genetically code a plant to repel pests, farmers don't have to spray with pesticides. That's what's meant by "replacing stuff with information."

I offer a prediction: the early twenty-first century is going to see a struggle between information technology and biotechnology on the one hand and environmental degradation on the other. Information technology is going to be our most powerful tool. It will let us miniaturize things, avoid waste, and produce more value without producing and processing more stuff. The substitution of information for stuff is essential to sustainability. (See "Monsanto's Smarter Products" at the end of this article.) Substituting services for products is another.

Explain what you mean by substituting services for products.

Bill McDonough, dean of the University of Virginia's School of Architecture in Charlottesville, made this come clear for me. He points out that we often buy things not because we want the things themselves but because we want what they can do. Television sets are an obvious example. No one says, "Gee, I'd love to put a cathode-ray tube and a lot of printed circuit boards in my living room." People *might* say, "I'd like to watch the ball game" or "Let's turn on the soaps." Another example: Monsanto makes nylon fiber, much of which goes into carpeting. Each year, nearly 2 million tons of old carpeting go into landfills, where they constitute about 1% of the entire U.S. municipal solid-waste load. Nobody really wants to own carpet; they just want to walk on it. What would happen if Monsanto or the carpet manufacturer owned that carpet and promised to come in and remove it when it required replacing? What would the economics of that look like? One of our customers is exploring that possibility today. It might be that if we got the carpet back, we could afford to put more cost into it in the first place in ways that would make it easier for us to recycle. Maybe then it wouldn't end up in a landfill.

Substituting services for products is one solution. Selling a carpet service instead of a carpet could be more sustainable.

We're starting to look at all our products and ask,
What is it people really need to buy? Do they need the
stuff or just its function? What would be the economic
impact of our selling a carpet service instead of a carpet?

Can you cite other examples of how we can replace stuff with information?

Sure. Information technology, whether it's telecommunications or virtual reality—whatever that turns out to
be—can eliminate the need to move people and things
around. In the past, if you wanted to send a document
from one place to another, it involved a lot of trains and
planes and trucks. Sending a fax eliminates all that
motion. Sending E-mail also eliminates the paper.

I have to add that any powerful new technology is
going to create ethical problems—problems of privacy,
fairness, ethics, power, or control. With any major
change in the technological substrate, society has to
solve those inherent issues.

You referred earlier to using information to miniatur-ize things. How does that work?

Miniaturization is another piece of sustainability
because it reduces the amount of stuff we use. There are
enormous potential savings in moving from very crude,
massive designs to smaller and more elegant ones.
Microelectronics is one example: the computing power
you have in your PC would have required an enormous
installation not many years ago.

We've designed things bigger than they need to be
because it's easier and because we thought we had
unlimited space and material. Now that we know we

don't, there's going to be a premium on smaller, smarter design. I think of miniaturization as a way to buy time. Ultimately, we'd love to figure out how to replace chemical processing plants with fields of growing plants—literally, green plants capable of producing chemicals. We have some leads: we can already produce polymers in soybeans, for example. But I think a big commercial breakthrough is a long way off.

Today, by developing more efficient catalysts, for example, we can at least make chemical plants smaller. There will be a number of feasible alternatives if we can really learn to think differently and set design criteria other than reducing immediate capital costs. One way is to design chemical plants differently. If you looked at life-cycle costs such as energy consumption, for instance, you would design a plant so that processes needing heat were placed next to processes generating heat; you wouldn't install as many heaters and coolers that waste energy. We think that if you really dig into your costs, you can accomplish a lot by simplifying and shrinking.

Some people are talking about breakthroughs in mechanical devices comparable to what's being done with electronic devices. Maybe the next wave will come through nanotechnology, but probably in 10 or 20 years, not tomorrow.

The key to sustainability, then, lies in technology?

I am not one of those techno-utopians who just assume that technology is going to take care of everyone. But I don't see an alternative to giving it our best shot.

Business leaders tend to trust technology and markets and to be optimistic about the natural unfolding of events. But at a visceral level, people know we are headed for trouble and would love to find a way to do something about it. The market is going to want sustainable systems, and if Monsanto provides them, we will do quite well for ourselves and our shareowners. Sustainable development is going to be one of the organizing principles around which Monsanto and a lot of other institutions will probably define themselves in the years to come.

Describe how you go about infusing this way of thinking into the company?

It's not hard. You talk for three minutes, and people light up and say, "Where do we start?" And I say, "I don't know. And good luck."

Maybe some context would help. We've been grappling with sustainability issues here long before we had a term for the concept. Part of our history as a chemical company is that environmental issues have been in our face to a greater extent than they've been in many other industries.

My predecessor, Dick Mahoney, understood that the way we were doing things had to change. Dick grew up, as I did not, in the chemical industry, so he tended to look at what was coming out of our plants. The publication of our first toxic-release inventory in 1988 galvanized attention around the magnitude of plant emissions.

Dick got way out ahead of the traditional culture in Monsanto and in the rest of the chemical industry. He set incredibly aggressive quantitative targets and deadlines. The first reaction to them was, My God, he must be out of his mind. But it was an effective technique. In six years, we reduced our toxic air emissions by 90%.

Not having "grown up in the chemical industry," as you put it, do you think differently about environmental issues?

Somewhat. Dick put us on the right path. We have to reduce—and ultimately eliminate—the negative impacts we have on the world. There is no argument on that subject. But even if Monsanto reached its goal of zero impact next Tuesday, that wouldn't solve the world's problem. Several years ago, I sensed that there was something more required of us than doing no harm, but I couldn't articulate what that was.

So I did what you always do. I got some smart people together—a group of about 25 critical thinkers, some of the company's up-and-coming leaders—and sent them off to think about it. We selected a good cross-section—some business-unit leaders, a couple from the management board, and people from planning, manufacturing, policy, and safety and health. And we brought in some nontraditional outsiders to challenge our underlying assumptions about the world. My request to this group was, "Go off, think about what's happening to the world, and come back with some recommendations about what it means for Monsanto. Do we have a role to play? If so, what is it?"

That off-site meeting in 1994 led to an emerging insight that we couldn't ignore the changing global environmental conditions. The focus around sustainable development became obvious. I should have been able to come up with that in about 15 minutes. But it took a group of very good people quite a while to think it through, to determine what was real and what was just puff, to understand the data, and to convince themselves that this wasn't a fluffy issue—and that we ought to be engaged in it.

People came away from that meeting emotionally fired up. It wasn't just a matter of Okay, you threw me an interesting business problem, I have done the analysis, here is the answer, and now can I go back to work. People came away saying, "Damn it, we've got to get going on this. This is important." When some of your best people care intensely, their excitement is contagious.

So now we have a bunch of folks engaged, recognizing that we have no idea where we're going to end up. No one—not the most sophisticated thinker in the world—can describe a sustainable world with 10 billion to 12 billion people, living in conditions that aren't disgusting and morally impermissible. But we can't sit around waiting for the finished blueprint. We have to start moving in directions that make us less unsustainable.

How are you doing that?

There's a quote of Peter Drucker's—which I will mangle here—to the effect that at some point strategy has to degenerate into work. At Monsanto, there was a flurry of E-mail around the world, and in a matter of four months a group of about 80 coalesced. Some were chosen; many others just heard about the project and volunteered. They met for the first time in October 1995 and decided to organize into seven teams: three focused on developing tools to help us make better decisions, three focused externally on meeting world needs, and one focused on education and communication. (See "Monsanto's Seven Sustainability Teams at the end of this article.")

We realized that many of the things we were already doing were part of a sustainability strategy even if we didn't call it that. We'd been working on pollution prevention and investing in biotechnology for years before we thought about the concept of sustainability. As we made more progress in pollution prevention, it became easier for everyone to grasp how pollution—or waste—actually represents a resource that's lost. When you translate that understanding into how you run a business, it leads to cost reduction. You can ask, did we do it because it reduces our costs or because of sustainability? That would be hard to answer because optimizing resources has become part of the way we think. But having the sustainability framework has made a difference, especially in how we weigh new business opportunities.

Can you give me some examples?

One of the seven sustainability teams is discussing how to gain a deeper understanding of global water needs and whether we at Monsanto might meet some of those needs with our existing capabilities. That is an example of a conversation that might not have occurred—or might have occurred much later—if we weren't focused on sustainability. Agricultural water is becoming scarcer, and the salination of soils is an increasing problem. In California, for example, they do a lot of irrigation, and when the water evaporates or flushes through the soil, it leaves small amounts of minerals and salts. Over time, the build-up is going to affect the soil's productivity.

Should we address the water side of the problem? Or can we approach the issue from the plant side? Can we develop plants that will thrive in salty soil? Or can we create less thirsty plants suited to a drier environment? If we had plants that could adapt, maybe semidesert areas could become productive.

Another problem is drinking water. Roughly 40% of the people on earth don't have an adequate supply of fresh water. In the United States, we have a big infrastructure for cleaning water. But in developing countries that lack the infrastructure, there might be a business opportunity for in-home water-purification systems.

I realize this is still early in the process, but how do you know that you're moving forward?

One interesting measure is that we keep drawing in more people. We started off with 80; now we have almost 140. And a lot of this response is just one person after another saying, "I want to be involved, and this is the team I want to be involved in." It's infectious. That's the way most good business processes work. To give people a script and tell them, "Your part is on page 17; just memorize it" is an archaic way to run institutions that have to regenerate and re-create themselves. It's a dead end.

Today, in most fields I know, the struggle is about creativity and innovation. There is no script. You have some ideas, some activities, some exhortations, and some invitations, and you try to align what people believe and what people care about with what they're free to do. And you hope that you can coordinate them in ways that aren't too wasteful—or, better still, that they can self-coordinate. If an institution wants to be adaptive, it has to let go of some control and trust that people will work on the right things in the right ways. That has some obvious implications for the ways you select people, train them, and support them.

Would it be accurate to say that all of your sustainability teams have been self-created and self-coordinated?

Someone asked me recently whether this was a top-down exercise or a bottom-up exercise. Those don't sound like very helpful concepts to me. This is about *us*. What do *we* want to do? Companies aren't machines anymore. We have thousands of independent agents trying to self-coordinate because it is in their interest to do so.

There is no top or bottom. That's just a metaphor and not a helpful one. People say, Here is what I think. What do you think? Does that make sense to you? Would you like to try it? I believe we must see what ideas really win people's hearts and trust that those ideas will turn out to be the most productive.

People in large numbers won't give their all for protracted periods of time—with a cost in their overall lives—for an abstraction called a corporation or an idea called profit. People can give only to people. They can give to their coworkers if they believe that they're engaged together in an enterprise of some importance. They can give to society, which is just another way of saying they can give to their children. They can give if they believe that their work is in some way integrated into a whole life.

Historically, there has been a bifurcation between who we are and the work we do, as if who we are is outside our work. That's unhealthy, and most people yearn to integrate their two sides. Because of Monsanto's history as a chemical company, we have a lot of employees—good people—with a recurrent experience like this: their kids or their neighbors' kids or somebody at a cocktail party asks them what kind of work they do and then reacts in a disapproving way because of what they *think* we are at Monsanto. And that hurts. People don't want to be made to feel ashamed of what they do.

I don't mean to disparage economic motives—they're obviously important. But working on sustainability offers a huge hope for healing the rift between our economic

activity and our total human activity. Instead of seeing
the two in Marxist opposition, we see them as the same
thing. Economics is part of human activity.

What are the organizational implications of that?

Part of the design and structure of any successful institution is going to be giving people permission to select
tasks and goals that they care about. Those tasks have to
pass some kind of economic screen; but much of what
people care about will pass because economic gain
comes from meeting people's needs. That's what
economies are based on.

The people who have been working on sustainability
here have done an incredible job, not because there has
been one presiding genius who has organized it all and
told them what to do but because they want to get it
done. They care intensely about it and they organize
themselves to do it.

I don't mean to romanticize it, but, by and large, self-
regulating systems are probably going to be more productive than those based primarily on control loops.
There are some institutions that for a short period can
succeed as a reflection of the will and ego of a single person. But they're unlikely to survive unless other people
resonate with what that person represents.

We're going to have to figure out how to organize people in ways that enable them to coordinate their activities without wasteful and intrusive systems of control
and without too much predefinition of what a job is. My
own view is that as long as you have a concept called a
job, you're asking people to behave inauthentically;
you're asking people to perform to a set of expectations
that someone else created. People give more if they can

figure out how to control themselves, how to regulate themselves, how to contribute what they can contribute out of their own authentic abilities and beliefs, not out of somebody else's predetermination of what they're going to do all day.

How will you measure your progress toward sustainability? Do you have milestones?

For something at this early level of exploration, you probably want to rely for at least a year on a subjective sense of momentum. People usually know when they're going someplace, when they're making progress. There's a pace to it that says, yes, we're on the right track. After that, I would like to see some quantitative goals with dates and very macro budgets. As the teams begin to come to some conclusions, we will be able to ignite the next phase by setting some specific targets.

"If emerging economies have to relive the entire industrial revolution . . . I think it's all over."

This is so big and complicated that I don't think we're going to end up with a neat and tidy document. I don't think environmental sustainability lends itself to that.

As your activities globalize, does the issue of sustainability lead you to think differently about your business strategy in different countries or regions of the world?

The developing economies can grow by brute force, by putting steel in the ground and depleting natural resources and burning a lot of hydrocarbons. But a far better way to go would be for companies like Monsanto to transfer their knowledge and help those countries avoid the mistakes of the past. If emerging economies have to relive the entire industrial revolution with all its waste, its energy use, and its pollution, I think it's all over.

Can we help the Chinese, for example, leapfrog from preindustrial to postindustrial systems without having to pass through that destructive middle? At the moment, the signs aren't encouraging. One that is, however, is China's adoption of cellular phones instead of tons of stuff: telephone poles and copper wire.

The fact that India is one of the largest software-writing countries in the world is encouraging. You'd like to see tens of millions of people in India employed in information technology rather than in making more stuff. But there's an important hurdle for companies like Monsanto to overcome. To make money through the transfer of information, we depend on intellectual property rights, which let us reconcile environmental and economic goals. As the headlines tell you, that's a little problematic in Asia. And yet it's critically important to our being able to figure out how to be helpful while making money. Knowledge transfer will happen a lot faster if people get paid for it.

Will individual companies put themselves at risk if they follow sustainable practices and their competitors don't?

I can see that somebody could get short-term advantage by cutting corners. As a matter of fact, the world economy *has* seized such an advantage—short-term in the sense of 500 years—by cutting corners on some basic laws of physics and thermodynamics. But it's like asking if you can gain an advantage by violating laws. Yes, I suppose you can—until they catch you. I don't think it is a good idea to build a business or an economy around the "until-they-catch-you principle." It can't be the right way to build something that is going to endure.

The multinational corporation is an impressive invention for dealing with the tension between the application of broadly interesting ideas on the one hand and economic and cultural differences on the other. Companies like ours have gotten pretty good at figuring out how to operate in places where we can make a living while remaining true to some fundamental rules. As more countries enter the world economy, they are accepting—with greater or lesser enthusiasm—that they are going to have to play by some rules that are new for them. My guess is that, over time, sustainability is going to be one of those rules.

Doesn't all this seem far away for managers? Far enough in the future for them to think, "It won't happen on my watch?"

The tension between the short term and the long term is one of the fundamental issues of business—and of life—and it isn't going to go away. Many chief executives have gotten where they are in part because they have a time horizon longer than next month. You don't stop caring about next month, but you also have to think further ahead. What's going to happen next in my world? If your world is soft drinks, for example, you have to ask where your clean water will come from.

How do you react to the prospect of the world population doubling over the next few decades? First you may say, Great, 5 billion more customers. That is what economic development is all about. That's part of it. Now, keep going. Think about all the physical implications of serving that many new customers. And ask yourself the hard question, How exactly are we going to do that and still live here? That's what sustainability is about.

I'm fascinated with the concept of distinctions that transform people. Once you learn certain things—once you learn to ride a bike, say—your life has changed forever. You can't unlearn it. For me, sustainability is one of those distinctions. Once you get it, it changes how you think. A lot of our people have been infected by this way of seeing the world. It's becoming automatic. It's just part of who you are.

Monsanto's Smarter Products

SCIENTISTS AT MONSANTO are designing products that use information at the genetic or molecular level to increase productivity. Here are three that are on the market today.

The NewLeaf Potato

The NewLeaf potato, bioengineered to defend itself against the destructive Colorado potato beetle, is already in use on farms. Monsanto also is working on the NewLeaf Plus potato with inherent resistance to leaf virus, another common scourge. Widespread adoption of the product could eliminate the manufacture, transportation, distribution, and aerial application of millions of pounds of chemicals and residues yearly.

B.t. Cotton

In ordinary soil, microbes known as B.t. microbes occur naturally and produce a special protein that, although toxic to certain pests, are harmless to other insects, wildlife, and people. If the destructive cotton budworm, for example, eats B.t. bacteria, it will die.

Some cotton farmers control budworms by applying to their cotton plants a powder containing B.t. But the powder often blows or washes away, and reapplying it is expensive. The alternative is for farmers to spray the field with a chemical insecticide as many as 10 or 12 times per season.

But Monsanto's scientists had an idea. They identified the gene that tells the B.t. bacteria to make the special protein. Then they inserted the gene in the cotton plant to enable it to produce the protein on its own while remaining unchanged in other respects. Now when budworms attack, they are either repelled or killed by the B.t.

With products like B.t. cotton, farmers avoid having to buy and apply insecticides. And the environment is spared chemicals that are persistent in the soil or that run off into the groundwater.

Roundup Herbicide and No-Till Farming

Sustainability has become an important design criterion in Monsanto's chemically based products as well as in its bioengineered products. Building the right information

---

Why use all this to protect potatoes from insects and viruses when . . .

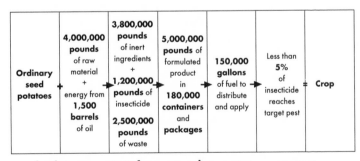

| Ordinary seed potatoes | + | 4,000,000 pounds of raw material + energy from 1,500 barrels of oil | → | 3,800,000 pounds of inert ingredients + 1,200,000 pounds of insecticide 2,500,000 pounds of waste | → | 5,000,000 pounds of formulated product in 180,000 containers and packages | → | 150,000 gallons of fuel to distribute and apply | → | Less than 5% of insecticide reaches target pest | = | Crop |

. . . built-in genetic information lets potatoes protect themselves?

| NewLeaf Plus seed potatoes | . . . . → | Crop |

into molecules, for example, can render them more durable or enhance their recyclability.

Roundup herbicide is a molecule designed to address a major problem for farmers: topsoil erosion. Topsoil is necessary for root systems because of its organic matter, friability in structure, and water-holding capabilities. The subsoil underneath is incapable of supporting root systems. Historically, farmers have tilled their soil primarily for weed control and only to a minor extent for seed preparation. But plowing loosens soil structure and exposes soil to erosion.

By replacing plowing with application of herbicides like Roundup—a practice called *conservation tillage*—farmers end up with better soil quality and less topsoil erosion. When sprayed onto a field before crop planting, Roundup kills the weeds, eliminating the need for plowing. And because the Roundup molecule has been designed to kill only what is growing at the time of its initial application, the farmer can come back a few days after spraying and begin planting; the herbicide will have no effect on the emerging seeds.

The Roundup molecule has other smart features that contribute to sustainability. It is degraded by soil microbes into natural products such as nitrogen, carbon dioxide, and water. It is nontoxic to animals because its mode of action is specific to plants. Once sprayed, it sticks to soil particles; it doesn't move into the groundwater. Like a smart tool, it seeks out its work.

Monsanto's Seven Sustainability Teams

THREE OF MONSANTO'S sustainability teams are working on tools and methodologies to assess, measure, and provide direction for internal management.

The Eco-efficiency Team

Because you can't manage what you don't measure, this team is mapping and measuring the ecological efficiency of Monsanto's processes. Team members must ask, In relation to the value produced, what inputs are consumed, and what outputs are generated? Managers have historically optimized raw material inputs, for example, but they have tended to take energy and water for granted because there is little financial incentive today to do otherwise. And although companies such as Monsanto have focused on toxic waste in the past, true eco-efficiency will require better measures of all waste. Carbon dioxide, for instance, may not be toxic, but it can produce negative environmental effects. Ultimately, Monsanto's goal is to pursue eco-efficiency in all its interactions with suppliers and customers.

The Full-Cost Accounting Team

This team is developing a methodology to account for the total cost of making and using a product during the product's life cycle, including the true environmental costs associated with producing, using, recycling, and disposing of it. The goal is to keep score in a way that doesn't eliminate from consideration all the environmental costs of what the company does. With better data, it will be possible to make smarter decisions today and as the underlying economics change in the future.

The Index Team

This team is developing criteria by which business units can measure whether or not they're moving toward sustainability. They are working on a set of metrics that balance economic, social, and environmental factors. Units will be able to track the sustainability of individual products and of whole businesses. These sustainability metrics will, in turn, be integrated into Monsanto's balanced-scorecard approach to the management of its businesses. The scorecard links and sets objectives for financial targets, customer satisfaction, internal processes, and organizational learning.

Three teams are looking externally to identify sustainability needs that Monsanto might address.

The New Business/New Products Team

This team is examining what will be valued in a marketplace that increasingly selects products and services that support sustainability. It is looking at areas of stress in natural systems and imagining how Monsanto's technological skills could meet human needs with new products that don't aggravate—that perhaps even repair—ecological damage.

The Water Team

The water team is looking at global water needs—a huge and growing problem. Many people don't have access to clean drinking water, and there is a worsening shortage of water for irrigation as well.

The Global Hunger Team

This team is studying how Monsanto might develop and deliver technologies to alleviate world hunger. That goal has been a core focus for the company for a number of years. For example, Monsanto had been studying how it might use its agricultural skills to meet people's nutritional needs in developing countries.

The final team develops materials and training programs.

The Communication and Education Team

This team's contribution is to develop the training to give Monsanto's 29,000 employees a common perspective. It offers a framework for understanding what sustainability means, how employees can play a role, and how they can take their knowledge to key audiences outside the company.

Originally published in January–February 1997
Reprint 97110

It's Not Easy Being Green

NOAH WALLEY AND

BRADLEY WHITEHEAD

Executive Summary

RESPONDING TO ENVIRONMENTAL problems has
always been a no-win proposition for managers. Help
the environment and hurt your business, or irreparably
harm your business while damaging the earth. Recently,
however, a new common wisdom has emerged that
promises the ultimate reconciliation of environmental and
economic concerns. In this new world, both business and
the environment can win. Being green is no longer a cost
of doing business; it is a catalyst for constant innovation,
new market opportunity, and wealth creation.

The proponents of this new popular wisdom cite a
mounting body of "win-win" projects that benefit the environment *and* create financial value. As an example, they
point to 3M's "Pollution Prevention Pays" program, a
group of over 3,000 mainly employee-generated projects, which, since 1975, have reduced 3M's emissions

by over one billion pounds while saving the company approximately $500 million.

The idea that a renewed interest in environmental management will result in increased profitability for business has widespread appeal. In this new green world, managers might redesign a product so that it uses fewer environmentally harmful or resource-depleting raw materials—an effort that if successful could result in considerable cuts in direct manufacturing costs and inventory savings.

This new vision sounds great, yet it is highly unrealistic. Environmental costs are skyrocketing at most companies, with little chance of economic payback in sight. Given this reality, McKinsey consultants Noah Walley and Bradley Whitehead ask whether or not win-win solutions should be the foundation of a company's environmental strategy.

For years, the goals of business and the environment seemed hopelessly irreconcilable. According to common wisdom, what helped one would almost certainly harm the other. Yet nearly a decade of "green" initiatives in the world's corporations has given rise to a more optimistic mind-set, which promises the ultimate reconciliation of environmental and economic concerns. In this new world, both business and the environment can win. Being green is no longer a cost of doing business; it is a catalyst for constant innovation, new market opportunity, and wealth creation.

Everyone from Vice President Al Gore to Harvard Business School Professor Michael Porter has sung the praises of being green. In fact, Gore argues, making environmental improvements is often the best way to increase a company's efficiency and, therefore, profitability. Gore and other proponents of this new popular wisdom cite an increasing number of projects that benefit the environment and create financial value. As an example of such a "win-win" project, Gore points to 3M's "Pollution Prevention Pays" program, a group of over 3,000 mainly employee-generated projects, which have reduced 3M's emissions by over 1 billion pounds since 1975 while saving the company approximately $500 million.

Questioning today's win-win rhetoric is like arguing against motherhood.

Questioning today's win-win rhetoric is akin to arguing against motherhood and apple pie. After all, the idea that environmental initiatives will systematically increase profitability has tremendous appeal. Unfortunately, this popular idea is also unrealistic. Responding to environmental challenges has always been a costly and complicated proposition for managers. In fact, environmental costs at most companies are skyrocketing, with little economic payback in sight.

In industries such as petroleum and chemicals, which are already plagued with overcapacity, fierce competition, and declining margins, a company's ability to respond to environmental challenges in a cost-efficient manner may well determine its viability. A major North American chemical company, for example, was enjoying an internal rate of return of 55% on employee-generated environmental initiatives similar to the win-win opportunities Gore cites. But when those impressive returns were added to the internal rate of return on *all* corporate environmental projects, the return dropped to a negative 16%.

We do not argue that win-win situations do not exist; in fact, they do, but they are very rare and will likely be overshadowed by the total cost of a company's environmental program. Win-win opportunities become insignificant in the face of the enormous environmental expenditures that will never generate a positive financial return.

Texaco, for example, plans to invest $1.5 billion per year over a five-year period on environmental compliance and emission reductions for a total investment of over $7 billion, an amount three times the book value of the company and twice its asset base. In other words, the company plans to double its asset base on projects expected to provide little, if any, revenues. Can anyone argue convincingly that an investment of this magnitude will yield a positive financial return to shareholders? We doubt it.

We must question the current euphoric environmental rhetoric by asking if win-win solutions should be the foundation of a company's environmental strategy. At the risk of arguing against motherhood (and mother earth) we must answer no. Ambitious environmental goals have real economic costs. As a society, we may rightly choose those goals despite their costs, but we must do so knowingly. And we must not kid ourselves. Talk is cheap; environmental efforts are not.

But just because environmental managers should not continue to search exclusively for win-win solutions does not mean that they should return to their old ways of fighting, ignoring, and hamstringing any and all environmental regulatory efforts. On the contrary, being conscious of shareholder value while protecting the environment requires, among other things, a deep understanding of the environmental and strategic consequences of business decisions, collaboration with environmental groups and regulators, involvement in shaping legislation (and even avoiding the need for it), and a sincere commitment to cleaning up and preventing pollution. The challenge for managers today is knowing how to pick the shots that will have the greatest impact. To achieve truly sustainable environmental solutions, managers must concentrate on finding smarter and finer trade-offs between business and environmental concerns, acknowledging that, in almost all cases, it is impossible to get something for nothing.

Concentrating on enhancing the efficiency and effectiveness of environmental spending may not have the rhetorical appeal of the current win-win talk, but in the long run, such an approach will be far more effective. Consider DuPont, which has the equivalent of 35% of its share price invested in capital and operating expenditures related to protecting the environment. Rather than searching for elusive, but virtuous, win-win situations, DuPont can protect shareholder value more successfully by finding ways to improve its long-term environmental efficiency. A 15% improvement in efficiency, for instance, could yield nearly $3 per share.

Other companies in pollution-intensive industries would see similar results from efforts to improve environmental efficiency. We estimate that between one-quarter and one-half of an industry's market value is vulnerable to increased environmental costs. And while it is difficult to know how much value will *actually* be destroyed by the increased cost of environmental compliance, it is clear that managers face a daunting task. The recently reauthorized Clean Air Act, for example, is expected to cost U.S. petroleum refiners $37 billion, over $6 billion more than the book value of the entire industry. And stories like that will likely multiply. McKinsey & Company's 1991 worldwide survey of several hundred executives, *The Corporate Response to the Environmental Challenge*, shows that top managers expect environmental expenditures to double as a percentage of sales over the next decade.

Given that scenario, companies should seek to minimize the destruction of shareholder value that is likely to be caused by environmental costs rather than attempt to create value through environmental enhancements. Indeed, the current win-win rhetoric is not just misleading; it is dangerous. In an area like the environment, which requires long-term commitment and cooperation, untempered idealism is a luxury. By focusing on the laudable but illusory goal of win-win solutions, corporations and policymakers are setting themselves up for a fall with shareholders and the public at large. Both constituencies will become cynical, disappointed, and uncooperative when the true costs of being green come to light. Companies are already beginning to question their public commitment to the environment, especially since such costly obligations often come at a time when many companies are undergoing dramatic expense restructurings and layoffs.

Evolving Eras of Environmental Management

The history of the complex relationship between business and the environment illuminates the appeal as well as the considerable danger of the win-win approach. As professors Kurt Fischer and Johan Schot outline in their introduction to *Environmental Strategies for Industry*, the current approach to environmental management developed in two eras over two decades, beginning in the early 1970s.

In the first era, which lasted from roughly 1970 to 1985, companies faced with new regulations of high technical specificity did little more than comply with the regulations and often fought or stymied them. Fischer and Schot accurately describe this phase as one of "resistant adaptation." During this period, companies were generally unwilling to internalize environmental issues, a reluctance that was reflected in the delegation of environmental protection to local facilities, a widespread failure to create environmental performance-measurement systems, and a refusal to view environmental issues as realities that needed to be incorporated into business strategy.

During the mid to late 1980s, a shift in the regulatory context and the maturing of the environmental movement created an incentive for managers to look beyond the narrow, predominantly technical approach. With regulations focused more on ultimate environmental results and less on the mechanics of compliance, managers began to exercise greater discretion in their environmental response. For the first time, environmental strategy became possible.

Fischer and Schot call this second phase "embracing environmental issues without innovating." Because corporate response in the first era was minimal and grudging, companies were able to make easy, but often very significant, improvements in the second era. Between 1989 and 1991, for example, Texaco achieved a 40% reduction in its combined air, water, and solid-waste streams and a 58% reduction in its toxic emissions through pollution-control equipment, tighter monitoring and control systems, and the introduction of an improved waste-reduction process. Similarly, between 1988 and 1992, Georgia-Pacific secured a 65% reduction in dioxins and a 34% decrease in chloroform emissions by relying on substitute chemicals, upgraded equipment, and improved process controls.

The emergence of the win-win mind-set is a direct result of the extraordinary success companies achieved in reducing pollution in this second era. Many of the reduction programs made good financial sense, while few required truly fundamental changes in production processes or product designs. Anxious to demonstrate their commitment to environmental progress, companies were quick to tout their successes. Even informed observers easily came to the conclusion that continued environmental action could more than pay for itself.

Why Win-Win Won't Work

In a foreword to the new edition of *Earth in the Balance*, Vice President Al Gore writes, "[W]e can prosper by leading the environmental revolution and producing for the world marketplace the new products and technologies that foster economic progress without environmental destruction." While Gore focuses primarily on government's role, he clearly believes that many win-win opportunities exist for corporations and that trade-offs can largely be avoided through smart decision making and technological innovation.

In his brief but influential *Scientific American* article, Harvard Business School Professor Michael Porter echoes Gore's view, arguing that the perceived conflict between environmental protection and economic competitiveness is, in fact, a false dichotomy. "Strict environmental regulations do not inevitably hinder competitive advantage against foreign rivals; indeed, they often enhance it," Porter writes. "Properly constructed regulatory standards, which aim at outcomes and not methods, will encourage companies to

Who wouldn't like to believe that concern for the environment will revive the country's economic and competitive outlook?

re-engineer their technology. The result in many cases is a process that not only pollutes less but lowers costs or improves quality."

In Gore and Porter's world, managers might redesign a product so that it uses fewer environmentally harmful or resource-depleting raw materials. If successful, that effort could also result in significant cuts in direct manufacturing costs and inventory savings and appeal to consumers' growing desire for environmentally friendly products.

That argument, with its rabbit-out-of-the-hat solutions to many environmental and economic ills, is certainly appealing. Who wouldn't be enamored of an approach that promises that a renewed concern for the environment will revive the country's economic and competitive outlook? Gore's book and Porter's persuasive arguments have unleashed—or at least reinforced—a school of thought that denies the necessity of trade-offs and encourages companies to pursue prosperity through green initiatives.

Yet while Gore and Porter give an inspirational rallying cry, they offer little specific guidance to managers. Porter writes mainly about how a country can gain competitive advantage through strict environmental policies, not about how individual companies might actually seek to gain competitive advantage by becoming green. But that hasn't stopped environmentalists from seizing on Porter's argument and urging businesses to capture the many opportunities to help the environment that await them.

Win-win rhetoric already pervades popular opinion. An April 1993 Times Mirror-Roper poll shows that over two-thirds of Americans do not believe the country must choose between environmental protection and economic development. Yet those who extrapolate a specific strategy for industry from Porter's argument are wrongly assuming that the recent spate of easy environmental wins can be carried on indefinitely. While tough environmental standards may yield significant positive results for the economy as a whole, individual companies will actually be battling increasingly complex environmental problems at a much higher cost than ever before.

Managers are realizing that all their relatively easy environmental problems have already been solved.

For example, one large chemical company, anxious to capitalize on its early successes, committed to a program to reduce emissions of hazardous wastes. The company soon found that it was starving other important projects, like plant upgrades, and that roughly two-thirds of its capital budget went to environmental spending. Perhaps even more alarming, nearly 80% of plant engineers' time was being consumed by environmental projects. Managers at this company are just beginning to understand that all their relatively easy environmental problems have already been solved and that the economic forces at work in the industry are making it increasingly difficult to find win-win solutions. The company is now exploring ways to achieve greater efficiency and perhaps even to reduce some of its commitments to the environment. As environmental challenges become more complex and costs continue to skyrocket, win-win solutions will become increasingly scarce. Environmental costs have stubbornly continued to outpace both inflation and economic growth for the past two decades. Between 1972 and 1992, for instance, total annualized environmental protection costs for the United States tripled as a percentage of gross domestic product (GDP) from 0.88% to 2.39%, with a further increase to 2.47%, or around $200 billion, projected by the year 2000. In pollution-intensive sectors like oil and gas, the problem is much worse. Compound annual growth in environmental expenditures for a selection of oil and gas companies between 1987 and 1990 was 12.9%, compared with only 7.3% for employee benefits (including health care) and 2.7% for direct labor charges.

Costs are destined to increase even more, especially since the increase in regulations shows no signs of abating. One crude but indicative proxy is that the number of federal environmental acts in force has risen from 5 in 1972 to over 40 today, a spate of legislative activity that has been responsible for a twelvefold increase in the number of pages of federal environmental regulation over the same period. By 1992, Title 40 of the Federal Code contained over 12,000 pages of regulations. And several pieces of environmental legislation, such as the Clean Water Act and the Resources Conservation and Recovery Act, are currently on the congressional docket.

Even without additional regulations, however, progressively tighter standards within current regulations will push corporate environmental spending higher. For example, nitrogen oxides standards (which cover a major air pollutant that often comes from the coal burned to generate electricity) were originally set by the Clean Air Act at a limit of 0.5 pounds per million British thermal units (BTUs) for electric utilities. This standard was subsequently superseded by many states with tighter limits, culminating in a 0.2 pounds per million BTUs standard to be achieved by 1999, which will result in a tenfold cost increase. While it may be possible to respond creatively to each new environmental regulation or enforcement, the burden on corporations is tremendous.

Moreover, within industries, the burden falls unevenly among companies. In the top ten companies in the oil industry, reported environmental expenditures vary from 5.1% to 1.3% of sales over a three-year period—a difference of roughly $800 million. And in steel, minimills enjoy a $10 to $15 environmental cost-per-ton advantage over traditional integrated producers.

Complicating the situation for environmental managers is the growing array of choices they have for how and when they will respond to environmental pressures. Managers today have so many choices that they aren't always sure what to do. Old-fashioned command-and-control regulations, which allow managers very little freedom, are giving way to market-based incentives, including tradable permits, pollution charges, and deposit refund systems. These new incentives do not tell a company what to do but instead provide a clear set of financial incentives that are designed to influence behavior positively, much like a capital market.

The result? Senior managers must frequently juggle a number of issues without a means for setting priorities or a method for integrating those issues into business decision making. In McKinsey's survey, 92% of CEOs and board members stated that the environment should be one of their top three management priorities, and 85% claimed that one of their major goals should be to integrate environmental considerations into business strategy. At the same time, only 37% believed they successfully integrate the environment into everyday operations, and only 35% said they successfully adapt business strategy to anticipated environmental developments.

The Search for Solutions

Clearly, today's managers lack a framework that will allow them to turn their good intentions into reality. A number of executives are attempting to do just that. Among the most practical of those is Swiss industrialist Stephan Schmidheiny, who led the Business Council at the 1992 Earth Summit in Rio de Janeiro. In *Changing Course*, Schmidheiny and his colleagues at the Business Council, including ABB Chairman Percy Barnevik, retired 3M Chairman and CEO Allen Jacobson, Dow Chemical President and CEO Frank Popoff, and Nippon Steel Chairman Akira Miki, articulate a vision of "sustainable development," or the ability to meet the needs of the present generation without compromising the welfare of future generations. The authors do not claim that growth and the environment are mutually reinforcing. Rather, they argue that economic growth and environmental protection are inextricably linked.

The vision they offer is based on free trade, market prices that reflect the comprehensive societal impact of products and processes, more flexible regulations, and investors who pay greater heed to environmental considerations. In the cases Schmidheiny cites, he shows a clear understanding of the environmental issues managers must face. Yet *Changing Course* does not, nor does it aspire to, provide an all-encompassing framework for managers who must daily negotiate the conflicting demands of the market and the environment.

Schmidheiny leaves CEOs with no clear guideposts for which products or processes to work on first and how far to go in cleaning up and at what cost. Without that guidance, even the most environmentally sensitive CEO will be lost. The current crop of environmental texts suggests that competitive advantage can be found in effective environmental management, yet these texts offer only one-dimensional prescriptions. The common rallying cry of many environmental thinkers is that the environment must be integrated into everyday business decisions, yet few specify what that means.

Many corporations view the environment as a discrete functional area generating issues that are treated in isolation from "core" business issues. Writers on all ends of the spectrum, however, now agree that the outmoded functional approach must yield to a more integrated way of thinking.

In her book *Costing the Earth,* Frances Cairncross, the environment editor of *The Economist,* suggests that the total quality movement may be one vehicle through which environmental issues can be integrated into business as a whole. "In American management terms," she writes, "environmental responsibility has become an aspect of the search for total quality."

In a world where you can't do everything, only a value-based approach allows informed trade-offs.

While Cairncross may be correct, most total quality environmental-management programs have a missionary focus on emissions reductions that doesn't take into account the cost at which that quality is obtained or, alternatively, the value created. Traditional cost-reduction efforts, on the other hand, err too much in the opposite direction by concentrating on quarterly costs without devoting sufficient attention to environmental impact and the longer term costs and liabilities.

The Path to Pragmatism

Instead of focusing on win-win solutions, companies would be better off focusing on the "trade-off zone," where environmental benefit is weighed judiciously against value destruction. Only a focus on value rather than compliance, emissions, or quarterly costs can provide managers with the information to set priorities and develop appropriate business responses. This does not mean that managers should obstruct environmental regulatory efforts. Instead, managers must pick their shots carefully. In a world where you cannot do everything, only a value-based approach allows informed trade-offs between costs and benefits.

Much work remains to define all the elements of a value-based approach. Broadly speaking, such an approach must be systematic, integrated, and flexible. Managers must set clear priorities based on the potential impact on shareholder value and the amount of discretion they have to deal with the environmental problem at hand; they must make environmental decisions in the context of the company's needs and strategy; and they must be able to exercise different options as an uncertain future unfolds.

Within this framework, environmental issues can be broken down into three broad categories: strategic, operational, and technical. (See the chart, "A Triage of Environmental Issues.") Each type requires a distinct managerial approach. Together they represent a way of thinking about the environment that goes beyond incremental, reactive, and functional approaches, which are now reaching the limits of their cost-effectiveness.

Some environmental issues are *strategic* because their impact on value is high enough either to put core elements of the business at risk or to fundamentally alter a company's cost structure, and because managers have considerable discretion about how to respond. A good example is the issue of chlorine-free paper production facing the pulp and paper industry. Opinion is sharply divided on when, and even whether, government regulation will prohibit the use of chlorine in the paper manu-

A Triage of Environmental Issues

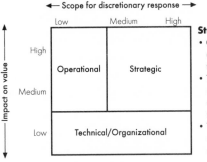

Operational Issues:
- Objectives and requirements are clear.
- There is limited uncertainty about the future.
- Substantial value can ride on the quality with which a solution is implemented.

← Scope for discretionary response →

	Low	Medium	High
High	Operational	Strategic	
Medium			
Low	Technical/Organizational		

Impact on value

Strategic Issues:
- Objectives are unclear and need to be set.
- There is considerable uncertainty about the future.
- The competitive ramifications are serious.

Technical/Organizational Issues:
- Degree of discretion varies from high to low, but relatively little value is tied up with any individual issue.
- The challenge is to configure the organization so that it can manage myriad issues without top management involvement.

facturing process. The value implications for pulp and paper companies are enormous, not only because of the absolute cost of chlorine-free production but also because some companies are likely, by virtue of their plant configuration or other reasons, to enjoy a relative competitive advantage in this form of manufacture. Meanwhile, the level of discretion in how to respond is considerable. While Louisiana-Pacific has started to prepare its organization for chlorine-free paper production, many other industry participants are fighting tooth and nail to undermine proposed legislation.

As that situation suggests, one key decision managers must make about each major environmental problem they face is whether to lead or lag behind their competitors on environmental issues. In some cases, a company will want to pursue an environmental strategy in which it gets well in front of regulations or public opinion, as Louisiana-Pacific did. In other cases, a corporation may be best served by moving in lockstep with industry leaders or reacting only in response to external pressures. The decision to lead or lag regulations is something of a management catch-22. If a company lags, it may find itself on the receiving end of unfavorable regulations, but if the company leads, its actions could increase near-term production costs and leave the company vulnerable to its competitors.

Managers will find that their options can be broken down into those that help them shape events, like forming partnerships with stake-holders, and those that help them develop an optimal response to events, like reallocating resource dollars and redesigning production processes. To prepare a strategy, managers must decide where they want to be on the spectrum from strict compliance to environmental leadership.

Operational issues are those where the impact on value ranges from medium to high, but managers' scope for discretionary response is generally low. Management's task with these issues is to ensure that minimum expenditures achieve maximum environmental impact. The example of broad emissions control, again from the pulp and paper industry, illustrates the point. While annual expenditures for complying with regulations controlling air, water, and solid-waste emissions are measured in the hundreds of millions of dollars, companies often have little choice about whether or how to comply.

The challenge with these issues is to view environmental costs as manageable, not as a set of mandates for which a blank check is the only solution. The first step is understanding how much is being spent on emission control and why. The second step is devising an approach that ensures that maximum environmental impact is achieved at minimum cost.

Finally, there are those issues that are largely *technical*, where the degree of managerial discretion varies from high to low, but relatively little value is tied up with any individual issue. The cumulative weight of thousands of these decisions, however, can have an adverse effect on shareholder value. Managers must have the necessary information to make informed trade-offs between cost and environmental control. Business unit managers seldom have adequate information about even current environmental costs let alone possible future liabilities or pressures. The best way to provide that information is to create systems to track and disseminate emissions data on a cross-functional basis, provide environmental cost accounting, and perform thorough, opportunity-oriented—as opposed to compliance-oriented—third-party audits. That approach is in contrast to current "worst practice," prevalent in the McKinsey survey, which can be summed up with this attitude: "There are enough problems that will find us without our having to find new ones."

For all environmental issues, shareholder value, rather than compliance, emissions, or costs, is the critical unifying metric. That approach is environmentally sound, but it's also hardheaded, informed by business experience, and, as a result, much more likely to be *truly* sustainable over the long term.

Suggested Readings

The Corporate Response to the Environmental Challenge (Amsterdam: McKinsey & Company, 1991).

Kurt Fischer and Johan Schot, *Environmental Strategies for Industry: International Perspectives on Research Needs and Policy Implications* (Washington, D.C.: Island Press, 1993).

Al Gore, *Earth in the Balance: Ecology and the Human Spirit* (New York: Penguin, 1993).

Michael E. Porter, "America's Green Strategy," *Scientific American,* April 1991.

Second Annual National Environment Survey by Times Mirror Magazines and the Roper Organization. Interviews of 1,005 adults nationwide conducted between April 2 and 8, 1993.

Stephan Schmidheiny with the Business Council for Sustainable Development, *Changing Course: A Global Business Perspective on Development and the Environment* (Cambridge, Mass.: MIT Press, 1992).

Frances Cairncross, *Costing the Earth: The Challenge for Governments, the Opportunities for Business* (Boston: Harvard Business School Press, 1992).

Originally published in May–June 1994
Reprint 94310

Beyond Greening

Strategies for a Sustainable World

STUART L. HART

Executive Summary

THREE DECADES into the environmental revolution, many companies in the industrialized nations have recognized that they can reduce pollution and increase profits at the same time. But beyond corporate "greening" lies the enormous challenge—and opportunity to develop a sustainable global economy, one that the planet is capable of supporting indefinitely.

Stuart Hart, director of the Corporate Environmental Management Program at the University of Michigan School of Business, explains the imperative of sustainable development and provides a framework for identifying the business opportunities behind sustainability. The dangers today are clear: exploding population growth, rapid depletion of resources, and ever more industrialization and urbanization are creating a terrible environmental burden.

105

Companies normally frame greening in terms of risk reduction, reengineering, or cost cutting. But, says Hart, when greening becomes part of strategy, opportunities of potentially staggering proportions open up. A number of companies are moving in that direction. BASF, for example, is colocating plants to make the recycling of waste feasible, and Xerox is reusing parts from leased copiers on new machines.

Hart identifies three stages of environmental strategy: pollution prevention, product stewardship, and the development of clean technology. But companies will not benefit from such efforts unless they draw a road map that can show them how new products and services must evolve and what competencies they will need. Businesses that create a vision of sustainability will be ready to take advantage of the opportunities presented by the need for a sustainable global economy.

THE ENVIRONMENTAL REVOLUTION has been almost three decades in the making, and it has changed forever how companies do business. In the 1960s and 1970s, corporations were in a state of denial regarding their impact on the environment. Then a series of highly visible ecological problems created a groundswell of support for strict government regulation. In the United States, Lake Erie was dead. In Europe, the Rhine was on fire. In Japan, people were dying of mercury poisoning.

Today many companies have accepted their responsibility to do no harm to the environment. Products and production processes are becoming cleaner; and where such change is under way, the environment is on the mend. In the industrialized nations, more and more companies are "going green" as they realize that they can reduce pollution and increase profits simultaneously. We have come a long way.

But the distance we've traveled will seem small when, in 30 years, we look back at the 1990s. Beyond greening lies an enormous challenge—and an enormous opportunity. The challenge is to develop a *sustainable global economy*: an economy that the planet is capable of supporting indefinitely. Although we may be approaching ecological recovery in the developed world, the planet as a whole remains on an unsustainable course. Those who think that sustainability is only a matter of pollution control are missing the bigger picture. Even if all the companies in the developed world were to achieve zero emissions by the year 2000, the earth would still be stressed beyond what biologists refer to as its carrying capacity. Increasingly, the scourges of the late twentieth century—depleted farmland, fisheries, and forests; choking urban pollution; poverty; infectious disease; and migration—are spilling over geopolitical borders. The simple fact is this: in meeting our needs, we are destroying the ability of future generations to meet theirs.

The roots of the problem—explosive population growth and rapid economic development in the emerging economies—are political and social issues that exceed the mandate and the capabilities of any corporation. At the same time, corporations are the only organizations with the resources, the technology, the global reach, and, ultimately, the motivation to achieve sustainability.

It is easy to state the case in the negative: faced with impoverished customers, degraded environments, failing political systems, and unraveling societies, it will be increasingly difficult for corporations to do business. But the positive case is even more powerful. The more we learn about the challenges of sustainability, the clearer it is that we are poised at the threshold of a historic moment in which many of the world's industries may be transformed.

To date, the business logic for greening has been largely operational or technical: bottom-up pollution-prevention programs have saved companies billions of dollars. However, few executives realize that environmental opportunities might actually become a major source of *revenue growth*. Greening has been framed in terms of risk reduction, reengineering, or cost cutting. Rarely is greening linked to strategy or technology development, and as a result, most companies fail to recognize opportunities of potentially staggering proportions.

Worlds in Collision

The achievement of sustainability will mean billions of dollars in products, services, and technologies that barely exist today. Whereas yesterday's businesses were often oblivious to their negative impact on the environment and today's responsible businesses strive for zero impact, tomorrow's businesses must learn to make a positive impact. Increasingly, companies will be selling solutions to the world's environmental problems.

Envisioning tomorrow's businesses, therefore, requires a clear understanding of those problems. To move beyond greening to sustainability, we must first unravel a complex set of global interdependencies. In fact, the global economy is really three different, overlapping economies.

The *market economy* is the familiar world of commerce comprising both the developed nations and the

emerging economies.[1] About a billion people—one-sixth
of the world's population—live in the developed countries of the market economy. Those affluent societies
account for more than 75% of the world's energy and
resource consumption and create the bulk of industrial,
toxic, and consumer waste. The developed economies
thus leave large ecological *footprints*—defined as the
amount of land required to meet a typical consumer's
needs. (See the exhibit "Ecological Footprints.")

Despite such intense use of energy and materials,
however, levels of pollution are relatively low in the
developed economies. Three factors account for this
seeming paradox: stringent environmental regulations,
the greening of industry, and the relocation of the most
polluting activities (such as commodity processing and
heavy manufacturing) to the emerging market
economies. Thus to some extent the greening of the
developed world has been at the expense of the environments in emerging economies. Given the much larger
population base in those countries, their rapid industri-

Ecological Footprints

 **United States**

 **The Netherlands**

 India

In the United States, it takes 12.2 acres to supply the average person's basic needs;
in the Netherlands, 8 acres; in India, 1 acre. The Dutch ecological footprint covers 15
times the area of the Netherlands, whereas India's footprint exceeds its area by only
about 35%. Most strikingly, if the entire world lived like North Americans, it would take
three planet Earths to support the present world population.

Source: Donella Meadows, "Our 'Footprints' Are Treading Too Much Earth," *Charleston (W.V.)*
Gazette, April 1, 1996.

alization could easily offset the environmental gains made in the developed economies. Consider, for example, that the emerging economies in Asia and Latin America (and now Eastern Europe and the former Soviet Union) have added nearly 2 billion people to the market economy over the past 40 years.

With economic growth comes urbanization. Today one of every three people in the world lives in a city. By 2025, it will be two out of three. Demographers predict that by that year there will be well over 30 megacities with populations exceeding 8 million and more than 500 cities with populations exceeding 1 million. Urbanization on this scale presents enormous infrastructural and environmental challenges.

Because industrialization has focused initially on commodities and heavy manufacturing, cities in many emerging economies suffer from oppressive levels of pollution. Acid rain is a growing problem, especially in places where coal combustion is unregulated. The World Bank estimates that by 2010 there will be more than 1 billion motor vehicles in the world. Concentrated in cities, they will double current levels of energy use, smog precursors, and emissions of greenhouse gas.

The second economy is the *survival economy*: the traditional, village-based way of life found in the rural parts of most developing countries. It is made up of 3 billion people, mainly Africans, Indians, and Chinese who are subsistence oriented and meet their basic needs directly from nature. Demographers generally agree that the world's population, currently growing by about 90 million people per year, will roughly double over the next 40 years. The developing nations will account for 90% of that growth, and most of it will occur in the survival economy.

Owing in part to the rapid expansion of the market economy, existence in the survival economy is becoming increasingly precarious. Extractive industries and infrastructure development have, in many cases, degraded the ecosystems upon which the survival economy depends. Rural populations are driven further into poverty as they compete for scarce natural resources. Women and children now spend on average four to six hours per day searching for fuelwood and four to six hours per week drawing and carrying water. Ironically, those conditions encourage high fertility rates because, in the short run, children help the family to garner needed resources. But in the long run, population growth in the survival economy only reinforces a vicious cycle of resource depletion and poverty.

Short-term survival pressures often force these rapidly growing rural populations into practices that cause long-term damage to forests, soil, and water. When wood becomes scarce, people burn dung for fuel, one of the greatest—and least well-known—environmental hazards in the world today. Contaminated drinking water is an equally grave problem. The World Health Organization estimates that burning dung and drinking contaminated water together cause 8 million deaths per year.

As it becomes more and more difficult to live off the land, millions of desperate people migrate to already overcrowded cities. In China, for example, an estimated 120 million people now roam from city to city, landless and jobless, driven from their villages by deforestation, soil erosion, floods, or droughts. Worldwide, the number of such "environmental refugees" from the survival economy may be as high as 500 million people, and the figure is growing.

The third economy is *nature's economy*, which consists of the natural systems and resources that support
the market and the survival economies. Nonrenewable
resources, such as oil, metals, and other minerals, are
finite. Renewable resources, such as soils and forests,
will replenish themselves—as long as their use does not
exceed critical thresholds. (See "Aracruz Celulose: A
Strategy for the Survival Economy" at the end of this
article.)

Technological innovations have created substitutes
for many commonly used nonrenewable resources; for
example, optical fiber now replaces copper wire. And in
the developed economies, demand for some virgin materials may actually diminish in the decades ahead
because of reuse and recycling. Ironically, the greatest
threat to sustainable development today is depletion of
the world's *renewable* resources.

Forests, soils, water, and fisheries are all being pushed
beyond their limits by human population growth and
rapid industrial develop-
ment. Insufficient fresh
water may prove to be the
most vexing problem in the
developing world over the
next decade, as agricul-
tural, commercial, and residential uses increase. Water
tables are being drawn down at an alarming rate, especially in the most heavily populated nations, such as
China and India.

*Increasingly, companies
will sell solutions
to the world's
environmental problems.*

Soil is another resource at risk. More than 10% of the
world's topsoil has been seriously eroded. Available
cropland and rangeland are shrinking. Existing crop
varieties are no longer responding to increased use of

fertilizer. As a consequence, per capita world production of both grain and meat peaked and began to decline during the 1980s. Meanwhile, the world's 18 major oceanic fisheries have now reached or actually exceeded their maximum sustainable yields.

By some estimates, humankind now uses more than 40% of the planet's net primary productivity. If, as projected, the population doubles over the next 40 years, we may outcompete most other animal species for food, driving many to extinction. In short, human activity now exceeds sustainability on a global scale. (See the exhibit "Major Challenges to Sustainability.")

As we approach the twenty-first century, the interdependence of the three economic spheres is increasingly evident. In fact, the three economies have become worlds in collision, creating the major social and environmental challenges facing the planet: climate change, pollution, resource depletion, poverty, and inequality.

Consider, for example, that the average American today consumes 17 times more than his or her Mexican counterpart (emerging economy) and hundreds of times more than the average Ethiopian (survival economy). The levels of material and energy consumption in the United States require large quantities of raw materials and commodities, sourced increasingly from the survival economy and produced in emerging economies.

In the survival economy, massive infrastructure development (for example, dams, irrigation projects, highways, mining operations, and power generation projects), often aided by agencies, banks, and corporations in the developed countries, has provided access to raw materials. Unfortunately, such development has often had devastating consequences for nature's economy and has tended to strengthen existing political and economic elites, with little benefit to those in the survival economy.

At the same time, infrastructure development projects have contributed to a global glut of raw materials and hence to a long-term fall in commodity prices. And as commodity prices have fallen relative to the prices of manufactured goods, the currencies of developing countries have weakened and their terms of trade have become less favorable. Their purchasing power declines while their already substantial debt load becomes even larger. The net effect of this dynamic has been the transfer of vast amounts of wealth (estimated at $40 billion per year since 1985) from developing to developed countries, producing a vicious cycle of resource exploitation and pollution to service mounting debt. Today develop-

Major Challenges to Sustainability

	Pollution	Depletion	Poverty
Developed economies	• greenhouse gases • use of toxic materials • contaminated sites	• scarcity of materials • insufficient reuse and recycling	• urban and minority unemployment
Emerging economies	• industrial emissions • contaminated water • lack of sewage treatment	• overexploitation of renewable resources • overuse of water for irrigation	• migration to cities • lack of skilled workers • income inequality
Survival economies	• dung and woodburning • lack of sanitation • ecosystem destruction due to development	• deforestation • overgrazing • soil loss	• population growth • low status of women • dislocation

ing nations have a combined debt of more than $1.2 trillion, equal to nearly half of their collective gross national product.

Strategies for a Sustainable World

Nearly three decades ago, environmentalists such as Paul Ehrlich and Barry Commoner made this simple but powerful observation about sustainable development: the total environmental burden (EB) created by human activity is a function of three factors. They are population (P); affluence (A), which is a proxy for consumption; and technology (T), which is how wealth is created. The product of these three factors determines the total environmental burden. It can be expressed as a formula: $EB = P \times A \times T$.

Achieving sustainability will require stabilizing or reducing the environmental burden. That can be done by decreasing the human population, lowering the level of affluence (consumption), or changing fundamentally the technology used to create wealth. The first option, lowering the human population, does not appear feasible short of draconian political measures or the occurrence of a major public-health crisis that causes mass mortality.

The second option, decreasing the level of affluence, would only make the problem worse, because poverty and population growth go hand in hand: demographers have long known that birth rates are inversely correlated with level of education and standard of living. Thus stabilizing the human population will require improving the education and economic standing of the world's poor, particularly women of childbearing age. That can be accomplished only by creating wealth on a massive scale. Indeed, it may be necessary to grow the world economy as much as tenfold just to provide basic amenities to a population of 8 billion to 10 billion.

That leaves the third option: changing the technology used to create the goods and services that constitute the world's wealth. Although population and consumption may be societal issues, technology is the business of business.

If economic activity must increase tenfold over what it is today just to provide the bare essentials to a population double its current size, then technology will have to improve twentyfold merely to keep the planet at its current levels of environmental burden. Those who believe that ecological disaster will somehow be averted must also appreciate the commercial implications of such a belief: over the next decade or so, sustainable development will constitute one of the biggest opportunities in the history of commerce.

Nevertheless, as of today few companies have incorporated sustainability into their strategic thinking. Instead, environmental strategy consists largely of piecemeal projects aimed at controlling or preventing pollution. Focusing on sustainability requires putting business strategies to a new test. Taking the entire planet as the context in which they do business, companies must ask whether they are part of the solution to social and environmental problems or part of the problem. Only when a company thinks in those terms can it begin to develop a vision of sustainability—a shaping logic that goes beyond today's internal, operational focus on greening to a more external, strategic focus on sustainable development. Such a vision is needed to guide companies through three stages of environmental strategy.

STAGE ONE: POLLUTION PREVENTION

The first step for most companies is to make the shift from pollution control to pollution prevention. Pollution control means cleaning up waste after it has been created. Pollution prevention focuses on minimizing or eliminating waste before it is created. Much like total quality management, pollution prevention strategies depend on continuous improvement efforts to reduce waste and energy use. This transformation is driven by a compelling logic: pollution prevention pays. Emerging global standards for environmental management systems (ISO 14,000, for example) also have created strong incentives for companies to develop such capabilities.

Over the past decade, companies have sought to avoid colliding with nature's economy (and incurring the associated added costs) through greening and prevention strategies. Aeroquip Corporation, a $2.5 billion manufacturer of hoses, fittings, and couplings, saw an opportunity here. Like most industrial suppliers, Aeroquip never thought of itself as a provider of environmental solutions. But in 1990, its executives realized that the company's products might be especially valuable in meeting the need to reduce waste and prevent pollution. Aeroquip has generated a $250 million business by focusing its attention on developing products that reduce emissions. As companies in emerging economies realize the competitive benefits of using raw materials and resources more productively, businesses like Aeroquip's will continue to grow.

Emerging economies cannot afford to repeat the mistakes of Western development.

The emerging economies cannot afford to repeat all the environmental mistakes of Western development. With the sustainability imperative in mind, BASF, the German chemical giant, is helping to design and build chemical industries in China, India, Indonesia, and Malaysia that are less polluting than in the past. By colocating facilities that in the West have been geographically dispersed, BASF is able to create industrial ecosystems in which the waste from one process becomes the raw material for another. Colocation solves a problem common in the West, where recycling waste is often infeasible because transporting it from one site to another is dangerous and costly.

STAGE TWO: PRODUCT STEWARDSHIP

Product stewardship focuses on minimizing not only pollution from manufacturing but also all environmental impacts associated with the full life cycle of a product. As companies in stage one move closer to zero emissions, reducing the use of materials and production of waste requires fundamental changes in underlying product and process design.

Design for environment (DFE), a tool for creating products that are easier to recover, reuse, or recycle, is becoming increasingly important. With DFE, all the effects that a product could have on the environment are examined during its design phase. Cradle-to-grave analysis begins and ends outside the boundaries of a company's operations—it includes a full assessment of all inputs to the product and examines how customers use and dispose of it. DFE thus captures a broad range of external perspectives by including technical staff, environmental experts, end customers, and even community representatives in the process. Dow Chemical Company has pioneered the use of a board-level advisory panel of environmental experts and external representatives to aid its product-stewardship efforts.

By reducing materials and energy consumption, DFE can be highly profitable. Consider Xerox Corporation's Asset Recycle Management (ARM) program, which uses leased Xerox copiers as sources of high-quality, low-cost parts and components for new machines. A well-developed infrastructure for taking back leased copiers combined with a sophisticated remanufacturing process allows parts and components to be reconditioned, tested, and then reassembled into "new" machines. Xerox estimates that ARM savings in raw materials, labor, and waste disposal in 1995 alone were in the $300-million to $400-million range. In taking recycling to this level, Xerox has reconceptualized its business. By redefining the product-in-use as part of the company's asset base, Xerox has discovered a way to add value and lower costs. It can continually provide its lease customers with the latest product upgrades, giving them state-of-the-art functionality with minimal environmental impact.

Product stewardship is thus one way to reduce consumption in the developed economies. It may also aid the quest for sustainability because developing nations often try to emulate what they see happening in the developed nations. Properly executed, product stewardship also offers the potential for revenue growth through product differentiation. For example, Dunlop Tire Corporation and Akzo Nobel recently announced a new radial tire that makes use of an aramid fiber belt rather than the conventional steel belt. The new design makes recycling easier because it eliminates the expensive cryogenic crushing required to separate the steel belts from the tire's other materials. Because the new fiber-belt tire is 30% lighter, it dramatically improves gas mileage. Moreover, it is a safer tire because it improves the traction control of antilock braking systems.

The evolution from pollution prevention to product stewardship is now happening in multinational companies such as Dow, DuPont, Monsanto, Xerox, ABB, Philips, and Sony. For example, as part of a larger sustainability strategy dubbed "A Growing Partnership with Nature," DuPont's agricultural-products business developed a new type of herbicide that has helped farmers around the world reduce their annual use of chemicals by more than 45 million pounds. The new Sulfonylurea herbicides have also led to a 1-billion-pound reduction in the amount of chemical waste produced in the manufacture of agricultural chemicals. These herbicides are effective at 1% to 5% of the application rates of traditional chemicals, are nontoxic to animals and nontarget species, and biodegrade in the soil, leaving virtually no residue on crops. Because they require so much less material in their manufacture, they are also highly profitable.

STAGE THREE: CLEAN TECHNOLOGY

Companies with their eye on the future can begin to plan for and invest in tomorrow's technologies. The simple fact is that the existing technology base in many industries is not environmentally sustainable. The chemical industry, for example, while having made substantial headway over the past decade in pollution prevention and product stewardship, is still limited by its dependence on the chlorine molecule. (Many organ-

ochlorides are toxic or persistent or bioaccumulative.)
As long as the industry relies on its historical competencies in chlorine chemistry, it will have trouble making
major progress toward sustainability.

Monsanto is one company that is consciously developing new competencies. It is shifting the technology
base for its agriculture business from bulk chemicals to
biotechnology. It is betting that the bioengineering of
crops rather than the application of chemical pesticides or fertilizers represents a sustainable path to
increased agricultural yields. (See Chapter 3, "Growth
Through Global Sustainability: An Interview with Monsanto's CEO, Robert B. Shapiro.")

Clean technologies are desperately needed in the
emerging economies of Asia. Urban pollution there has
reached oppressive levels. But precisely because manufacturing growth is so high—capital stock doubles every
six years—there is an unprecedented opportunity to
replace current product and process technologies with
new, cleaner ones.

Japan's Research Institute for Innovative Technology
for the Earth is one of several new research and technology consortia focusing on the development and commercialization of clean technologies for the developing
world. Having been provided with funding and staff by
the Japanese government and more than 40 corporations, RITE has set forth an ambitious 100-year plan to
create the next generation of power technology, which
will eliminate or neutralize greenhouse gas emissions.

Sustainability Vision

Pollution prevention, product stewardship, and clean
technology all move a company toward sustainability.

But without a framework to give direction to those activities, their impact will dissipate. A vision of sustainability for an industry or a company is like a road map to the future, showing the way products and services must evolve and what new competencies will be needed to get there. Few companies today have such a road map. Ironically, chemical companies, regarded only a decade ago as the worst environmental villains, are among the few large corporations to have engaged the challenge of sustainable development seriously.

Companies can begin by taking stock of each component of what I call their *sustainability portfolio.* (See the exhibit "The Sustainability Portfolio.") Is there an overarching vision of sustainability that gives direction to the company's activities? To what extent has the company progressed through the three stages of environmental strategy—from pollution prevention to product stewardship to clean technology?

Without a framework for environmental activities, their impact will dissipate.

Consider the auto industry. During the 1970s, government regulation of tailpipe emissions forced the industry to focus on pollution control. In the 1980s, the industry began to tackle pollution prevention. Initiatives such as the Corporate Average Fuel Efficiency requirement and the Toxic Release Inventory led auto companies to examine their product designs and manufacturing processes in order to improve fuel economy and lower emissions from their plants.

The 1990s are witnessing the first signs of product stewardship. In Germany, the 1990 "take-back" law required auto manufacturers to take responsibility for their vehicles at the end of their useful lives. Innovators such as BMW have influenced the design of new cars with their *design for disassembly* efforts. Industry-level consortia such as the Partnership for a New Generation of Vehicles are driven largely by the product stewardship logic of lowering the environmental impact of automobiles throughout their life cycle.

The Sustainability Portfolio

	Internal	**External**
Tomorrow	*Clean technology* Is the environmental performance of our products limited by our existing competency base? Is there potential to realize major improvements through new technology?	*Sustainability vision* Does our corporate vision direct us toward the solution of social and environmental problems? Does our vision guide the development of new technologies, markets, products, and processes?
Today	*Pollution prevention* Where are the most significant waste and emission streams from our current operations? Can we lower costs and risks by eliminating waste at the source or by using it as useful input?	*Product stewardship* What are the implications for product design and development if we assume responsibility for a product's entire life cycle? Can we add value or lower costs while simultaneously reducing the impact of our products?

This simple diagnostic tool can help any company determine whether its strategy is consistent with sustainability. First, assess your company's capability in each of the four quadrants by answering the questions in each box. Then rate yourself on the following scale for each quadrant: 1–nonexistent; 2–emerging; 3–established; or 4–institutionalized.

Most companies will be heavily skewed toward the lower left-hand quadrant, reflecting investment in pollution prevention. However, without investments in the future technologies and markets (the upper half of the portfolio), the company's environmental strategy will not meet evolving needs.

Unbalanced portfolios spell trouble, a bottom-heavy portfolio suggests a good position today but future vulnerability. A top-heavy portfolio indicates a vision of sustainability without the operational or analytical skills needed to implement it. A portfolio skewed to the left side of the chart indicates a preoccupation with handling the environmental challenge through internal process improvements and technology-development initiatives. Finally, a portfolio skewed to the right side, although highly open and public, runs the risk of being labeled a "greenwash" because the underlying plant operations and core technology still cause significant environmental harm.

Early attempts to promote clean technology include such initiatives as California's zero-emission vehicle law and the U.N. Climate Change Convention, which ultimately will limit greenhouse gases on a global scale. But early efforts by industry incumbents have been either incremental—for example, natural-gas vehicles—or defensive in nature. Electric-vehicle programs, for instance, have been used to demonstrate the infeasibility of this technology rather than to lead the industry to a fundamentally cleaner technology.

Although the auto industry has made progress, it falls far short of sustainability. For the vast majority of auto companies, pollution prevention and product stewardship are the end of the road. Most auto executives assume that if they close the loop in both production and design, they will have accomplished all the necessary environmental objectives.

But step back and try to imagine a sustainable vision for the industry. Growth in the emerging markets will generate massive transportation needs in the coming decades. Already the rush is on to stake out positions in China, India, and Latin America. But what form will this opportunity take?

Consider the potential impact of automobiles on China alone. Today there are fewer than 1 million cars on the road in China. However, with a population of more than 1 billion, it would take less than 30% market penetration to equal the current size of the U.S. car market (12 million to 15 million units sold per year). Ultimately, China might demand 50 million or more units annually. Because China's energy and transportation infrastructures are still being defined, there is an opportunity to develop a clean technology yielding important environmental and competitive benefits.

Amory Lovins of the Rocky Mountain Institute has demonstrated the feasibility of building *hypercars*—vehicles that are fully recyclable, 20 times more energy efficient, 100 times cleaner, and cheaper than existing cars. These vehicles retain the safety and performance of conventional cars but achieve radical simplification through the use of lightweight, composite materials, fewer parts, virtual prototyping, regenerative braking, and very small, hybrid engines. Hypercars, which are more akin to computers on wheels than to cars with microchips, may render obsolete most of the competencies associated with today's auto manufacturing—for example, metal stamping, tool and die making, and the internal combustion engine.

Assume for a minute that clean technology like the hypercar or Mazda's soon-to-be-released hydrogen rotary engine can be developed for a market such as China's. Now try to envision a transportation infrastructure capable of accommodating so many cars. How long will it take before gridlock and traffic jams force the auto industry to a halt? Sustainability will require new transportation solutions for the needs of emerging economies with huge populations. Will the giants in the auto industry be prepared for such radical change, or will they leave the field to new ventures that are not encumbered by the competencies of the past?

A clear and fully integrated environmental strategy should not only guide competency development, it should also shape the company's relationship to customers, suppliers, other companies, policymakers, and all its stakeholders. Companies can and must change the way customers think by creating preferences for products and services consistent with sustainability. Companies must become educators rather than mere marketers of products. (See the exhibit "Building Sustainable Business Strategies.")

For senior executives, embracing the quest for sustainability may well require a leap of faith. Some may feel that the risks associated with investing in unstable and unfamiliar markets outweigh the potential benefits. Others will recognize the power of such a positive mission to galvanize people in their organizations.

Regardless of their opinions on sustainability, executives will not be able to keep their heads in the sand for long. Since 1980, foreign direct investment by multinational corporations has increased from $500 billion to nearly $3 trillion per year. In fact, it now exceeds official development-assistance aid in developing countries. With free trade on the rise, the next decade may see the figure increase by another order of magnitude. The challenges presented by emerging markets in Asia and Latin America demand a new way of conceptualizing business

Building Sustainable Business Strategies

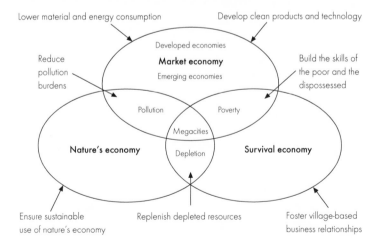

opportunities. The rapid growth in emerging economies cannot be sustained in the face of mounting environmental deterioration, poverty, and resource depletion. In the coming decade, companies will be challenged to develop clean technologies and to implement strategies that drastically reduce the environmental burden in the developing world while simultaneously increasing its wealth and standard of living.

Like it or not, the responsibility for ensuring a sustainable world falls largely on the shoulders of the world's enterprises, the economic engines of the future. Clearly, public policy innovations (at both the national and international levels) and changes in individual consumption patterns will be needed to move toward sustainability. But corporations can and should lead the way, helping to shape public policy and driving change in consumers' behavior. In the final analysis, it makes good business sense to pursue strategies for a sustainable world.

Aracruz Celulose: A Strategy for the Survival Economy

"POVERTY IS ONE OF THE WORLD'S leading polluters," notes Erling Lorentzen, founder and chairman of Aracruz Celulose. The $2 billion Brazilian company is the world's largest producer of eucalyptus pulp. "You can't expect people who don't eat a proper meal to be concerned about the environment."[1]

From the very start, Aracruz has been built around a vision of sustainable development. Lorentzen understood that building a viable forest-products business in Brazil's impoverished and deforested state of Espirito Santo would require the simultaneous improvement of nature's economy and the survival economy.

First, to restore nature's economy, the company took advantage of a tax incentive for tree planting in the late 1960s and began buying and reforesting cut-over land. By 1992, the company had acquired over 200,000 hectares and planted 130,000 hectares with managed eucalyptus; the rest was restored as conservation land. By reforesting what had become highly degraded land, unsuitable for agriculture, the company addressed a fundamental environmental problem. At the same time, it created a first-rate source of fiber for its pulping operations. Aracruz's forest practices and its ability to clone seedlings have given the company advantages in both cost and quality.

Aracruz has tackled the problem of poverty head-on. Every year, the company gives away millions of eucalyptus seedlings to local farmers. It is a preemptive strategy, aimed at reducing the farmers' need to deplete the natural forests for fuel or lumber. Aracruz also has a long-term commitment to capability building. In the early years, Aracruz was able to hire local people for very low wages because of their desperate situation. But instead of simply exploiting the abundant supply of cheap labor, the company embarked on an aggressive social-investment strategy, spending $125 million to support the creation of hospitals, schools, housing, and a training center for employees. In fact, until recently, Aracruz spent more on its social investments than it did on wages (about $1.20 for every $1 in wages). Since that time, the standard of living has improved dramatically, as has productivity. The company no longer needs to invest so heavily in social infrastructure.

1. Marguerite Rigoglioso, "Stewards of the Seventh Generation," *Harvard Business School Bulletin*, April 1996, p. 55.

Note

1. The terms *market economy, survival economy,* and
   nature's economy were suggested to me by Vandana
   Shiva, *Ecology and the Politics of Survival* (New Delhi:
   United Nations University Press, 1991).

Originally published in January–February 1997
Reprint 97105

Green *and* Competitive

Ending the Stalemate

MICHAEL E. PORTER AND
CLAAS VAN DER LINDE

Executive Summary

THE LINGERING BELIEF THAT environmental regulations
erode competitiveness has resulted in a stalemate. One
side pushes for tougher standards, the other tries to roll
standards back. The prevailing view is that there is an
inherent and fixed trade-off: ecology versus the economy.
On one side are the social benefits that arise from environmental standards. On the other side are the private costs
to industry of prevention and cleanup that lead to higher
prices and reduced industrial competitiveness.

This static view, in which everything except regulation
is held constant, ignores the fact the companies are
constantly finding innovative solutions in response to pressures of all sorts—from competitors, from customers, from
regulators. The authors' research shows that tougher environmental standards can enhance competitiveness by
pushing companies to use resources more productively.

The concept of *resource productivity* opens up a new way of looking at this complex issue. Today managers and regulators focus on the actual costs of eliminating or treating pollution. To end the stalemate, they should focus instead on the enormous opportunity costs of pollution—wasted resources, wasted effort, and diminished product value to the customer. Managers must start to recognize environmental improvement as an economic and competitive opportunity, not as an annoying cost or an inevitable threat.

Environmental progress demands that companies innovate to raise resource productivity—precisely the new challenge of global competition. It is time to build on the underlying economic logic that links the environment, resource productivity, innovation, and competitiveness.

T HE NEED FOR REGULATION to protect the environment gets widespread but grudging acceptance: widespread because everyone wants a livable planet, grudging because of the lingering belief that environmental regulations erode competitiveness. The prevailing view is that there is an inherent and fixed trade-off: ecology versus the economy. On one side of the trade-off are the *social* benefits that arise from strict environmental standards. On the other are industry's *private* costs for prevention and cleanup—costs that lead to higher prices and reduced competitiveness. With the argument framed this way, progress on environmental quality has become a kind of arm wrestling match. One side pushes for tougher standards; the other tries to roll them back. The balance of power shifts one way or the other depending on the prevailing political winds.

This static view of environmental regulation, in which everything except regulation is held constant, is incorrect. If technology, products, processes, and customer needs were all fixed, the conclusion that regulation must raise costs would be inevitable. But companies operate in the real world of dynamic competition, not in the static world of much economic theory. They are constantly finding innovative solutions to pressures of all sorts— from competitors, customers, and regulators.

Properly designed environmental standards can trigger innovations that lower the total cost of a product or improve its value. Such innovations allow companies to use a range of inputs more productively—from raw materials to energy to labor—thus offsetting the costs of improving environmental impact and ending the stalemate. Ultimately, this enhanced *resource productivity* makes companies more competitive, not less.

Consider how the Dutch flower industry has responded to its environmental problems. Intense cultivation of flowers in small areas was contaminating the soil and groundwater with pesticides, herbicides, and fertilizers. Facing increasingly strict regulation on the release of chemicals, the Dutch understood that the only effective way to address the problem would be to develop a closed-loop system. In advanced Dutch greenhouses, flowers now grow in water and rock wool, not in soil. This lowers the risk of infestation, reducing the need for fertilizers and pesticides, which are delivered in water that circulates and is reused.

The tightly monitored closed-loop system also reduces variation in growing conditions, thus improving product quality. Handling costs have gone down because the flowers are cultivated on specially designed platforms. In addressing the environmental problem, then, the Dutch have innovated in ways that have raised the productivity with which they use many of the resources involved in growing flowers. The net result is not only dramatically lower environmental impact but also lower costs, better product quality, and enhanced global competitiveness. (See "Innovating to Be Competitive: The Dutch Flower Industry" at the end of this article.)

This example illustrates why the debate about the relationship between competitiveness and the environment has been framed incorrectly. Policy makers, business leaders, and environmentalists have focused on the static cost impacts of environmental regulation and have ignored the more important offsetting productivity benefits from innovation. As a result, they have acted too often in ways that unnecessarily drive up costs and slow down progress on environmental issues. This static mind-set has thus created a self-fulfilling prophecy leading to ever more costly environmental regulation. Regulators tend to set regulations in ways that deter innovation. Companies, in turn, oppose and delay regulations instead of innovating to address them. The whole process has spawned an industry of litigators and consultants that drains resources away from real solutions.

Pollution's hidden costs—wasted resources and effort—are buried throughout a product's life cycle.

Pollution = Inefficiency

Are cases like the Dutch flower industry the exception rather than the rule? Is it naive to expect that reducing pollution will often enhance competitiveness? We think not, and the reason is that pollution often is a form of economic waste. When scrap, harmful substances, or energy forms are discharged into the environment as pollution, it is a sign that resources have been used incompletely, inefficiently, or ineffectively. Moreover, companies then have to perform additional activities that add cost but create no value for customers: for example, handling, storage, and disposal of discharges. The concept of resource productivity opens up a new way of looking at both the full systems costs and the value associated with any product. Resource inefficiencies are most obvious within a company in the form of incomplete material utilization and poor process controls, which result in unnecessary waste, defects, and stored materials. But there also are many other hidden costs buried in the life cycle of the product. Packaging discarded by distributors or customers, for example, wastes resources and adds costs. Customers bear additional costs when they use products that pollute or waste energy. Resources are lost when products that contain usable materials are discarded and when customers pay—directly or indirectly—for product disposal.

The shift from pollution control to prevention is a good first step, but companies must go further.

Environmental improvement efforts have traditionally overlooked these systems costs. Instead, they have focused on pollution control through better identification, processing, and disposal of discharges or waste— costly approaches. In recent years, more advanced companies and regulators have embraced the concept of pollution prevention, sometimes called source reduction, which uses such methods as material substitution and closed-loop processes to limit pollution before it occurs.

But, although pollution prevention is an important step in the right direction, ultimately companies must learn to frame environmental improvement in terms of resource productivity.[1] Today managers and regulators focus on the actual costs of eliminating or treating pollution. They must shift their attention to include the opportunity costs of pollution—wasted resources, wasted effort, and diminished product value to the customer. At the level of resource productivity, environmental improvement and competitiveness come together.

This new view of pollution as resource inefficiency evokes the quality revolution of the 1980s and its most powerful lessons. Today we have little trouble grasping the idea that innovation can improve quality while actually lowering cost. But as recently as 15 years ago, managers believed there was a fixed trade-off. Improving quality was expensive because it could be achieved only through inspection and rework of the "inevitable" defects that came off the line. What lay behind the old view was the assumption that both product design and production processes were fixed. As managers have rethought the quality issue, however, they have abandoned that old mind-set. Viewing defects as a sign of inefficient product and process design—not as an inevitable by-product of manufacturing—was a breakthrough. Companies now strive to build quality into the entire process. The new mind-set unleashed the power of innovation to relax or eliminate what companies had previously accepted as fixed trade-offs.

Like defects, pollution often reveals flaws in the product design or production process. Efforts to eliminate pollution can therefore follow the same basic principles widely used in quality programs: Use inputs more efficiently, eliminate the need for hazardous, hard-to-handle materials, and eliminate unneeded activities. In a recent study of major process changes at ten manufacturers of printed circuit boards, for example, pollution-control personnel initiated 13 of 33 major changes. Of the 13 changes, 12 resulted in cost reduction, 8 in quality improvements, and 5 in extension of production capabilities.[2] It is not surprising that total quality management (TQM) has become a source of ideas for pollution reduction that can create offsetting benefits. The Dow Chemical Company, for example, explicitly identified the link between quality improvement and environmental performance by using statistical-process control to reduce the variance in processes and to lower waste.

Innovation and Resource Productivity

To explore the central role of innovation and the connection between environmental improvement and resource productivity, we have been collaborating since 1991 with the Management Institute for Environment and Business (MEB) on a series of international case studies of industries and sectors significantly affected by environmental regulation: pulp and paper, paint and coatings, electronics manufacturing, refrigerators, dry cell batteries, and printing inks. (See the table "Environmental Regulation Has Competitive Implications.") The data clearly show that the costs of addressing environmental regulations can be minimized, if not eliminated, through innovation that delivers other competitive benefits. We first observed the phenomenon in the course of our research for a study of national competitiveness, *The Competitive Advantage of Nations* (The Free Press, 1990).

Consider the chemical sector, where many believe that the ecology-economy trade-off is particularly steep.

Environmental Regulation Has Competitive Implications

Sector/industry	Environmental issues	Innovative solutions	Innovation offsets
Pulp and paper	Dioxin released by bleaching with chlorine	Improved cooking and washing processes Elimination of chlorine by using oxygen, ozone, or peroxide for bleaching Closed-loop processes (still problematic)	Lower operating costs through greater use of by-product energy sources 25% initial price premium for chlorine-free paper
Paint and coatings	Volatile organic compounds (VOCs) in solvents	New paint formulations (low-solvent-content paints, water-borne paints) Improved application techniques Powder or radiation-cured coatings	Price premium for solvent-free paints Improved coatings quality in some segments Worker safety benefits Higher coatings-transfer efficiency Reduced coating costs through materials savings
Electronics manufacturing	Volatile organic compounds (VOCs) in cleaning agents	Semiaqueous, terpene-based cleaning agents Closed-loop systems No-clean soldering where possible	Increase in cleaning quality and thus in product quality 30% to 80% reduction in cleaning costs, often for one-year payback periods Elimination of an unnecessary production step

Refrigerators	Chlorofluorocarbons (CFCs) used as refrigerants Energy usage Disposal	Alternative refrigerants (propane-isobutane mix) Thicker insulation Better gaskets Improved compressors	10% better energy efficiency at same cost 5% to 10% initial price premium for "green" refrigerator
Dry cell batteries	Cadmium, mercury, lead, nickel, cobalt, lithium, and zinc releases in landfills or to the air (after incineration)	Rechargeable batteries of nickel-hydride (for some applications) Rechargeable lithium batteries (now being developed)	Nearly twice as efficient at same cost Higher energy efficiency Expected to be price competitive in the near future
Printing inks	VOCs in petroleum inks	Water-based inks and soy inks	Higher efficiency, brighter colors, and better printability (depending on application)

Sources: Benjamin C. Bonifant, Ian Ratcliffe, and Claas van der Linde.

A study of activities to prevent waste generation at 29 chemical plants found innovation offsets that enhanced resource productivity. Of 181 of these waste prevention activities, only one resulted in a net cost increase. Of the 70 activities with documented changes in product yield, 68 reported increases; the average for 20 initiatives documented with specific data was 7%. These innovation offsets were achieved with surprisingly low investments and very short payback times. One-quarter of the 48 initiatives with detailed capital cost information required *no* capital investment at all; of the 38 initiatives with data on the payback period, nearly two-thirds recouped their initial investments in six months or less. The annual savings per dollar spent on source reduction averaged $3.49 for the 27 activities for which this information could be calculated. The study also found that the two main motivating factors for source reduction activities were waste disposal costs and environmental regulation.

Innovation in response to environmental regulation can fall into two broad categories. The first is new technologies and approaches that minimize the cost of dealing with pollution once it occurs. The key to these approaches often lies in taking the resources embodied in the pollution and converting them into something of value. Companies get smarter about how to process toxic materials and emissions into usable forms, recycle scrap, and improve secondary treatment. For example, at a Rhône-Poulenc plant in Chalampe, France, nylon by-products known as diacids used to be incinerated.

Innovating to meet regulations can bring offsets: using inputs better, creating better products, or improving product yields.

Rhône-Poulenc invested 76 million francs and installed new equipment to recover and sell these diacids as additives for dyes and tanning and as coagulation agents. The new recovery process has generated annual revenues of about 20.1 million francs. New de-inking technologies developed by Massachusetts-based Thermo Electron Corporation, among others, are allowing more extensive use of recycled paper. Molten Metal Technology of Waltham, Massachusetts, has developed a cost-saving catalytic extraction method to process many types of hazardous waste.

The second and far more interesting and important type of innovation addresses the root causes of pollution by improving resource productivity in the first place. Innovation offsets can take many forms, including more efficient utilization of particular inputs, better product yields, and better products. (See "Environmental Improvement Can Benefit Resource Productivity" at the end of this article.) Consider the following examples.

Resource productivity improves when less costly materials are substituted or when existing ones are better utilized. Dow Chemical's California complex scrubs hydrochloric gas with caustic to produce a wide range of chemicals. The company used to store the wastewater in evaporation ponds. Regulation called for Dow to close the evaporation ponds by 1988. In 1987, under pressure to comply with the new law, the company redesigned its production process. It reduced the use of caustic soda, decreasing caustic waste by 6,000 tons per year and hydrochloric acid waste by 80 tons per year. Dow also found that it could capture a portion of the waste stream for reuse as a raw material in other parts of the plant. Although it cost only $250,000 to implement, the process gave Dow an annual savings of $2.4 million.[3]

3M also improved resource productivity. Forced to comply with new regulations to reduce solvent emissions by 90%, 3M found a way to avoid the use of solvents altogether by coating products with safer, water-based solutions. The company gained an early-mover advantage in product development over competitors, many of whom switched significantly later. The company also shortened its time to market because its water-based product did not have to go through the approval process for solvent-based coatings.[4]

3M found that innovations can improve process consistency, reduce downtime, and lower costs substantially. The company used to produce adhesives in batches that were then transferred to storage tanks. One bad batch could spoil the entire contents of a tank. Lost product, downtime, and expensive hazardous-waste disposal were the result. 3M developed a new technique to run rapid quality tests on new batches. It reduced hazardous wastes by 110 tons per year at almost no cost, yielding an annual savings of more than $200,000.[5]

Many chemical-production processes require an initial start-up period after production interruptions in order to stabilize output and bring it within specifications. During that time, only scrap material is produced. When regulations raised the cost of waste disposal, Du Pont was motivated to install higher-quality monitoring equipment, which in turn reduced production interruptions and the associated production start-ups. Du Pont lowered not only its waste generation but also cut the amount of time it wasn't producing anything.[6]

Process changes to reduce emissions and use resources more productively often result in higher yields. As a result of new environmental standards, Ciba-Geigy Corporation reexamined the wastewater streams at its dye plant in Tom's River, New Jersey. Engineers made two changes to the production process. First, they replaced sludge-creating iron with a less harmful chemical conversion agent. Second, they eliminated the release of a potentially toxic product into the wastewater stream. They not only reduced pollution but also increased process yields by 40%, realizing an annual cost savings of $740,000. Although that part of the plant was ultimately closed, the example illustrates the role of regulatory pressure in process innovation.

Process innovations to comply with environmental regulation can even improve product consistency and quality. In 1990, the Montreal Protocol and the U.S. Clean Air Act required electronics companies to eliminate ozone-depleting chlorofluorocarbons (CFCs). Many companies used them as cleaning agents to remove residues that occur in the manufacture of printed circuit boards. Scientists at Raytheon confronted the regulatory challenge. Initially, they thought that complete elimination of CFCs would be impossible. After research, however, they found an alternate cleaning agent that could be reused in a closed-loop system. The new method improved average product quality—which the old CFC-based cleaning agent had occasionally compromised—while also lowering operating costs. Responding to the same regulation, other researchers identified applications that did not require any cleaning at all and developed so-called no-clean soldering technologies, which lowered operating costs without compromising quality. Without environmental regulation, that innovation would not have happened.

Innovations to address environmental regulations can also lower product costs and boost resource productivity by reducing unnecessary packaging or simplifying designs. A 1991 law in Japan set standards to make products easier to recycle. Hitachi, along with other Japanese appliance producers, responded by redesigning products to reduce disassembly time. In the process, it cut back the number of parts in a washing machine by 16% and the number of parts in a vacuum cleaner by 30%. Fewer components made the products easier not only to disassemble but also to assemble in the first place. Regulation that requires such recyclable products can lower the user's disposal costs and lead to designs that allow a company to recover valuable materials more easily. Either the customer or the manufacturer who takes back used products reaps greater value.

Although such product innovations have been prompted by regulators instead of by customers, world demand is putting a higher value on resource-efficient products. Many companies are using innovations to command price premiums for "green" products and to open up new market segments. Because Germany adopted recycling standards earlier than most other countries, German companies have first-mover advantages in developing less packaging-intensive products, which are both lower in cost and sought after in the marketplace. In the United States, Cummins Engine Company's development of low-emissions diesel engines for such applications as trucks and buses—innovation that U.S. environmental regulations spurred—is allowing it to gain position in international markets where similar needs are growing.

These examples and many others like them do not prove that companies always can innovate to reduce environmental impact at low cost. However, they show that there are considerable opportunities to reduce pollution through innovations that redesign products, processes, and methods of operation. Such examples are common in spite of companies' resistance to environmental regulation and in spite of regulatory standards that often are hostile to innovative, resource-productive solutions. The fact that such examples are common carries an important message: Today a new frame of reference for thinking about environmental improvement is urgently needed.

Do We Really Need Regulation?

If innovation in response to environmental regulation can be profitable—if a company can actually offset the cost of compliance through improving resource productivity—why is regulation necessary at all? If such opportunities exist, wouldn't companies pursue them naturally and wouldn't regulation be unnecessary? That is like saying there will rarely be ten-dollar bills to be found on the ground because someone already will have picked them up.

Certainly, some companies do pursue such innovations without, or in advance of, regulation. In Germany and Scandinavia, where both companies and consumers are very attuned to environmental concerns, innovation is not uncommon. As companies and their customers adopt the resource productivity mind-set and as knowledge about innovative technologies grows, there may well be less need for regulation over time in the United States.

But the belief that companies will pick up on profitable opportunities without a regulatory push makes a false assumption about competitive reality—namely, that all profitable opportunities for innovation have already been discovered, that all managers have perfect information about them, and that organizational incentives are aligned with innovating. In fact, in the real world, managers often have highly incomplete information and limited time and attention. Barriers to change are numerous. The Environmental Protection Agency's Green Lights program, which works with companies to promote energy-saving lighting, shows that many ten-dollar bills are still waiting to be picked up. In

Our research on competitiveness highlights the role that outside pressure plays in motivating companies to innovate.

one audit, nearly 80% of the projects offered paybacks within two years or less, and yet the companies considering them had not taken action.[7] Only after companies joined the program and benefited from the EPA's information and cajoling were such highly profitable projects implemented.

We are now in a transitional phase of industrial history in which companies are still inexperienced in handling environmental issues creatively. Customers, too, are unaware that resource inefficiency means that they must pay for the cost of pollution. For example, they tend to see discarded packaging as free because there is no separate charge for it and no current lower-cost alternative. Because there is no direct way to recapture the value of the wasted resources that customers already have paid for, they imagine that discarding used products carries no cost penalty for them.

Regulation, although a different type than is currently practiced, is needed for six major reasons:

- To create pressure that motivates companies to innovate. Our broader research on competitiveness highlights the important role of outside pressure in overcoming organizational inertia and fostering creative thinking.

• To improve environmental quality in cases in which innovation and the resulting improvements in resource productivity do not completely offset the cost of compliance; or in which it takes time for learning effects to reduce the overall cost of innovative solutions.

• To alert and educate companies about likely resource inefficiencies and potential areas for technological improvement (although government cannot know better than companies how to address them).

• To raise the likelihood that product innovations and process innovations in general will be environmentally friendly.

• To create demand for environmental improvement until companies and customers are able to perceive and measure the resource inefficiencies of pollution better.

• To level the playing field during the transition period to innovation-based environmental solutions, ensuring that one company cannot gain position by avoiding environmental investments. Regulation provides a buffer for innovative companies until new technologies are proven and the effects of learning can reduce technological costs.

Those who believe that market forces alone will spur innovation may argue that total quality management programs were initiated without regulatory intervention. However, TQM came to the United States and Europe through a different kind of pressure. Decades earlier, TQM had been widely diffused in Japan—the result of a whole host of government efforts to make product quality a national goal, including the creation of the Deming Prize. Only after Japanese companies had devastated them in the marketplace did Americans and Europeans embrace TQM.

The Cost of the Static Mind-Set

Regulators and companies should focus, then, on relaxing the trade-off between environmental protection and competitiveness by encouraging innovation and resource productivity. Yet the current adversarial climate drives up the costs of meeting environmental standards and circumscribes the innovation benefits, making the trade-off far steeper than it needs to be.

To begin with, the power struggle involved in setting and enforcing environmental regulations consumes enormous amounts of resources. A 1992 study by the Rand Institute for Civil Justice, for example, found that 88% of the money that insurers paid out between 1986 and 1989 on Superfund claims went to pay for legal and administrative costs, whereas only 12% was used for actual site cleanups.[8] The Superfund law may well be the most inefficient environmental law in the United States, but it is not the only cause of inefficiency. We believe that a substantial fraction of environmental spending as well as of the revenues of environmental

Businesses spend too many of their environmental dollars on fighting regulation and not enough on finding real solutions.

products and services companies relates to the regulatory struggle itself and not to improving the environment.

One problem with the adversarial process is that it locks companies into static thinking and systematically pushes industry estimates of the costs of regulation upward. A classic example occurred during the debate in the United States on the 1970 Clean Air Act. Lee Iacocca, then executive vice president of the Ford Motor Company, predicted that compliance with the new regulations would require huge price increases for automobiles, force U.S. production to a halt by 1975, and severely damage the U.S. economy. The 1970 Clean Air Act was subsequently enacted, and Iacocca's dire predictions turned out to be wrong. Similar stories are common.

Static thinking causes companies to fight environmental standards that actually could enhance their competitiveness. Most distillers of coal tar in the United States, for example, opposed 1991 regulations requiring substantial reductions in benzene emissions. At the time, the only solution was to cover the tar storage tanks with costly gas blankets. But the regulation spurred Aristech Chemical Corporation of Pittsburgh, Pennsylvania, to develop a way to remove benzene from tar in the first processing step, thereby eliminating the need for gas blankets. Instead of suffering a cost increase, Aristech saved itself $3.3 million.

Moreover, company mind-sets make the costs of addressing environmental regulations appear higher than they actually are. Many companies do not account for a learning curve, although the actual costs of compliance are likely to decline over time. A recent study in the pulp-and-paper sector, for example, found the actual costs of compliance to be $4 to $5.50 per ton, whereas original industry estimates had been as high as $16.40.[9] Similarly, the cost of compliance with a 1990 regulation controlling sulfur dioxide emissions is today only about half of what analysts initially predicted, and it is heading lower. With a focus on innovation and resource productivity, today's compliance costs represent an upper limit.

There is legitimate controversy over the benefits to society of specific environmental standards. Measuring the health and safety effects of cleaner air, for example, is the subject of ongoing scientific debate. Some believe that the risks of pollution have been overstated. But whatever the level of *social* benefits proves to be, the *private* costs to companies are still far higher than necessary.

Good Regulation Versus Bad

In addition to being high-cost, the current system of environmental regulation in the United States often deters innovative solutions or renders them impossible. The problem with regulation is not its strictness. It is the way in which standards are written and the sheer inefficiency with which regulations are administered. Strict standards can and should promote resource productivity. The United States' regulatory process has squandered this potential, however, by concentrating on cleanup instead of prevention, mandating specific technologies, setting compliance deadlines that are unrealistically short, and subjecting companies to unnecessarily high levels of uncertainty.

The current system discourages risk taking and experimentation. Liability exposure and the government's inflexibility in enforcement, among other things, contribute to the problem. For example, a company that innovates and achieves 95% of target emissions reduction while also registering substantial offsetting cost reductions is still 5% out of compliance and subject to liability. On the other hand, regulators would reward it for adopting safe but expensive secondary treatment. (See "Innovation-Friendly Regulation" at the end of this article.)

Just as bad regulation can damage competitiveness, good regulation can enhance it. Consider the differences between the U.S. pulp-and-paper sector and the Scandinavian. Strict early U.S. regulations in the 1970s were imposed without adequate phase-in periods, forcing companies to adopt best available technologies quickly. At that time, the requirements invariably meant installing proven but costly end-of-pipe treatment systems. In Scandinavia, on the other hand, regulation permitted more flexible approaches, enabling companies to focus on the production process itself, not just on secondary treatment of wastes. Scandinavian companies developed innovative pulping and bleaching technologies that not only met emission requirements but also lowered operating costs. Even though the United States was the first to regulate, U.S. companies were unable to realize any first-mover advantages because U.S. regulations ignored a critical principle of good environmental regulation: Create maximum opportunity for innovation by letting industries discover how to solve their own problems.

Bad regulation is damaging to competitiveness, but the right kind of regulation can enhance it.

Unfortunately for the U.S. pulp-and-paper industry, a second principle of good regulation was also ignored: Foster continuous improvement; do not lock in on a particular technology or the status quo. The Swedish regulatory agency took a more effective approach. Whereas the United States mandated strict emissions goals and established very tight compliance deadlines, Sweden started out with looser standards but clearly communicated that tougher ones would follow. The results were predictable. U.S. companies installed secondary treatment systems and stopped there. Swedish producers, anticipating stricter standards, continually incorporated innovative environmental technologies into their normal cycles of capacity replacement and innovation.

The innovation-friendly approach produced the residual effect of raising the competitiveness of the local equipment industry. Spurred by Scandinavian demand for sophisticated process improvements, local pulp-and-paper-equipment suppliers, such as Sunds Defibrator and Kamyr, ultimately made major international gains in selling innovative pulping and bleaching equipment.

Eventually, the Scandinavian pulp-and-paper industry was able to reap innovation offsets that went beyond those directly stemming from regulatory pressures. By the early 1990s, producers realized that growing public awareness of the environmental problems associated with pulp-mill effluents was creating a niche market. For a time, Scandinavian companies with totally chlorine-free paper were able to command significant price premiums and serve a rapidly growing market segment of environmentally informed customers.

German and Japanese car makers captured early-mover advantages, but U.S. car makers chose to fight regulations.

Implications for Companies

Certainly, misguided regulatory approaches have imposed a heavy burden on companies. But managers who have responded by digging in their heels to oppose all regulation have been shortsighted as well. It is no secret that Japanese and German automobile makers developed lighter and more fuel-efficient cars in response to new fuel consumption standards, while the less competitive U.S. car industry fought such standards and hoped they would go away. The U.S. car industry eventually realized that it would face extinction if it did not learn to compete through innovation. But clinging to the static mind-set too long cost billions of dollars and many thousands of jobs.

To avoid making the same mistakes, managers must start to recognize environmental improvement as an economic and competitive opportunity, not as an annoying cost or an inevitable threat. Instead of clinging to a perspective focused on regulatory compliance, companies need to ask questions such as What are we wasting? and How could we enhance customer value? The early movers—the companies that can see the opportunity first and embrace innovation-based solutions—will reap major competitive benefits, just as the German and Japanese car makers did. (See "The New Environmentalists" at the end of this article.)

At this stage, for most companies, environmental issues are still the province of outsiders and specialists. That is not surprising. Any new management issue tends to go through a predictable life cycle. When it first arises, companies hire outside experts to help them navigate. When practice becomes more developed, internal specialists take over. Only after a field becomes mature do companies integrate it into the ongoing role of line management.

Many companies have delegated the analysis of environmental problems and the development of solutions to outside lawyers and environmental consultants. Such experts in the adversarial regulatory process, who are not deeply familiar with the company's overall technology and operations, inevitably focus on compliance rather than innovation. They invariably favor end-of-pipe solutions. Many consultants, in fact, are associated with vendors who sell such technologies. Some companies are in the second phase, in which environmental issues are assigned to internal specialist—for example, legal, governmental-affairs, or environmental departments—lack full profit responsibility and are separate from the line organization. Again, the result is almost always narrow, incremental solutions.

If the sorts of process and product redesigns needed for true innovation are even to be considered, much less implemented, environmental strategies must become an issue for general management. Environmental impact must be embedded in the overall process of improving productivity and competitiveness. The resource-productivity model, rather than the pollution-control model, must govern decision making.

Companies that adopt the resource-productivity framework will reap the greatest benefits.

How can managers accelerate their companies' progress toward a more competitive environmental approach? First, they can measure their direct and indirect environmental impacts. One of the major reasons that companies are not very innovative about environmental problems is ignorance. A large producer of organic chemicals, for example, hired a consultant to explore waste reduction opportunities in its 40 waste streams. A careful audit uncovered 497 different waste streams—the company had been wrong by a factor of more than ten.[10] Our research indicates that the act of measurement alone leads to enormous opportunities to improve productivity.

Companies that adopt the resource-productivity framework and go beyond currently regulated areas will reap the greatest benefits. Companies should inventory all unused, emitted, or discarded resources or packaging. Within the company, some poorly utilized resources will be held within plants, some discharged, and some put in dumpsters. Indirect resource inefficiencies will occur at the level of suppliers, channels, and customers. At the customer level, resource inefficiencies show up in the use of the product, in discarded packaging, and in resources left in the used-up product.

Second, managers can learn to recognize the opportunity cost of underutilized resources. Few companies have analyzed the true cost of toxicity, waste, and what they discard, much less the second-order impacts that waste and discharges have on other activities. Fewer still look beyond the out-of-pocket costs of dealing with pollution to the opportunity cost of the resources they waste or the productivity they forgo. There are scarcely any companies that think about customer value and the opportunity cost of wasted resources at the customer level.

Many companies do not even track environmental spending carefully, and conventional accounting systems are ill equipped to measure underutilized resources. Companies evaluate environmental projects as discrete, stand-alone investments. Straightforward waste- or discharge-reduction investments are screened using high hurdle rates that presume the investments are risky—leaving ten-dollar bills on the ground. Better information and evaluation methods will help managers reduce environmental impact while improving resource productivity.

Third, companies should create a bias in favor of innovation-based, productivity-enhancing solutions. They should trace their own and their customers' discharges, scrap, emissions, and disposal activities back into company activities to gain insight about beneficial product design, packaging, raw material, or process changes. We have been struck by the power of certain systems solutions: Groups of activities may be reconfigured, or substitutions in inputs or packaging may enhance utilization and potential for recovery. Approaches that focus on treatment of discrete discharges should be sent back to the organization for rethinking.

Current reward systems are as anti-innovation as regulatory policies. At the plant level, companies reward output but ignore environmental costs and wasted resources. The punishment for an innovative, economically efficient solution that falls short of expectations is often far greater than the reward for a costly but "successful" one.

Finally, companies must become more proactive in defining new types of relationships with both regulators and environmentalists. Businesses need a new mind-set. How can companies argue shrilly that regulations harm competitiveness and then expect regulators and environmentalists to be flexible and trusting as those same companies request time to pursue innovative solutions?

The World Economy in Transition

It is time for the reality of modern competition to inform our thinking about the relationship between competitiveness and the environment. Traditionally, nations were competitive if their companies had access to the lowest cost inputs—capital, labor, energy, and raw materials. In industries relying on natural resources, for example, the competitive companies and countries were those with abundant local supplies. Because technology changed slowly, a comparative advantage in inputs was enough for success.

Today globalization is making the notion of comparative advantage obsolete. Companies can source low-cost inputs anywhere, and new, rapidly emerging technologies can offset disadvantages in the cost of inputs. Facing high labor costs at home, for example, a company can automate away the need for unskilled labor. Facing

Resisting innovation will lead to loss of competitiveness in today's global economy.

a shortage of a raw material, a company can find an alternative raw material or create a synthetic one. To overcome high space costs, Japanese companies pioneered just-in-time production and avoided storing inventory on the factory floor.

It is no longer enough simply to have resources. Using resources productively is what makes for competitiveness today. Companies can improve resource productivity by producing existing products more efficiently or by making products that are more valuable to customers—products customers are willing to pay more for. Increasingly, the nations and companies that are most competitive are not those with access to the lowest-cost inputs but those that employ the most advanced technology and methods in using their inputs. Because technology is constantly changing, the new paradigm of global competitiveness requires the ability to innovate rapidly.

This new paradigm has profound implications for the debate about environmental policy—about how to approach it, how to regulate, and how strict regulation should be. The new paradigm has brought environmental improvement and competitiveness together. It is important to use resources productively, whether those resources are natural and physical or human and capital. Environmental progress demands that companies innovate to raise resource productivity—and that is precisely what the new challenges of global competition demand. Resisting innovation that reduces pollution, as the U.S. car industry did in the 1970s, will lead not only to environmental damage but also to the loss of competitiveness in the global economy. Developing countries that stick with resource-wasting methods and forgo environmental standards because they are "too expensive" will remain uncompetitive, relegating themselves to poverty.

How an industry responds to environmental problems may, in fact, be a leading indicator of its overall competitiveness. Environmental regulation does not lead inevitably to innovation and competitiveness or to higher productivity for all companies. Only those companies that innovate successfully will win. A truly competitive industry is more likely to take up a new standard as a challenge and respond to it with innovation. An uncompetitive industry, on the other hand, may not be oriented toward innovation and thus may be tempted to fight all regulation.

It is not at all surprising that the debate pitting the environment against competitiveness has developed as it has. Indeed, economically destructive struggles over redistribution are the norm in many areas of public policy. But now is the time for a paradigm shift to carry us forward into the next century. International competition has changed dramatically over the last few decades. Senior managers who grew up at a time when environmental regulation was synonymous with litigation will see increasing evidence that environmental improvement is good business. Successful environmentalists, regulatory agencies, and companies will reject old trade-offs and build on the underlying economic logic that links the environment, resource productivity, innovation, and competitiveness.

Innovating to Be Competitive: The Dutch Flower Industry

THE DUTCH FLOWER INDUSTRY IS responsible for about 65% of world exports of cut flowers—an astonishing figure given that the most important production inputs in the flower business would seem to be land and climate. Anyone who has been to the Netherlands knows its disadvantages on both counts. The Dutch have to reclaim land from the sea, and the weather is notoriously problematic.

How can the Dutch be the world's leaders in the flower business when they lack comparative advantage in the traditional sense? The answer, among other reasons, is that they have innovated at every step in the value chain, creating technology and highly specialized inputs that enhance resource productivity and offset the country's natural disadvantages.

In selling and distribution, for example, the Netherlands has five auction houses custom designed for the flower business. Carts of flowers are automatically towed on computer-guided paths into the auction room. The buying process occurs in a few seconds. Buyers sit in an amphitheater, and the price on the auction clock moves down until the first buyer signals electronically. That buyer's code is attached to the cart, which is routed to the company's shipping and handling area. Within a few minutes, the flowers are on a truck to regional markets or in a specialized, precooled container on their way to nearby Schiphol airport. Good airports and highway systems may be plentiful elsewhere, too. But the Netherlands' innovative, specialized infrastructure is a competitive advantage. It leads to very high productivity. It is so successful that growers from other countries actually fly flowers there to be processed, sold, and reexported.

Paradoxically, having a *shortage* of general-purpose or more basic inputs can sometimes be turned into an advantage. If land were readily available and the climate more favorable, the Dutch would have competed the same way other countries did. Instead they were forced to innovate, developing a high-tech system of year-round greenhouse cultivation. The Dutch continually improve the unique, specialized technology that creates high resource productivity and underpins their competitiveness.

In contrast, an abundance of labor and natural resources or a lack of environmental pressure may lead a country's companies to spend the national resources unproductively. Competing based on cheap inputs, which could be used with less productivity, was sufficient in a more insular, less global economy. Today, when emerging nations with even cheaper labor and raw materials are part of the global economy, the old strategy is unsustainable.

Environmental Improvement Can Benefit Resource Productivity

Process Benefits

- materials savings resulting from more complete processing, substitution, reuse, or recycling of production inputs
- increases in process yields

- less downtime through more careful monitoring and maintenance
- better utilization of by-products
- conversion of waste into valuable forms
- lower energy consumption during the production process
- reduced material storage and handling costs
- savings from safer workplace conditions
- elimination or reduction of the cost of activities involved in discharges or waste handling, transportation, and disposal
- improvements in the product as a by-product of process changes (such as better process control)

Product Benefits

- higher quality, more consistent products
- lower product costs (for instance, from material substitution)
- lower packaging costs
- more efficient resource use by products
- safer products
- lower net costs of product disposal to customers
- higher product resale and scrap value

Innovation-Friendly Regulation

REGULATION, PROPERLY CONCEIVED, need not drive up costs. The following principles of regulatory design will promote innovation, resource productivity, and competitiveness:

Focus on outcomes, not technologies. Past regulations have often prescribed particular remediation technologies, such as catalysts or scrubbers for air pollution. The phrases "best available technology" (BAT) and "best available control technology" (BACT) are deeply rooted in U.S. practice and imply that one technology is best, discouraging innovation.

Enact strict rather than lax regulation. Companies can handle lax regulation incrementally, often with end-of-pipe or secondary treatment solutions. Regulation, therefore, needs to be stringent enough to promote real innovation.

Regulate as close to the end user as practical, while encouraging upstream solutions. This will normally allow more flexibility for innovation in the end product and in all the production and distribution stages. Avoiding pollution entirely or, second best, mitigating it early in the value chain is almost always less costly than late-stage remediation or cleanup.

Employ phase-in periods. Ample but well-defined phase-in periods tied to industry-capital-investment cycles will allow companies to develop innovative resource-saving technologies rather than force them to implement expensive solutions hastily, merely patching over problems. California imposed such short compliance deadlines on its wood-furniture industry that many manufacturers chose to leave the state rather than add costly control equipment.

Use market incentives. Market incentives such as pollution charges and deposit-refund schemes draw attention to resource inefficiencies. In addition, tradable permits provide continuing incentives for innovation and encourage creative use of technologies that exceed current standards.

Harmonize or converge regulations in associated fields. Liability exposure in the United States leads companies to stick to safe, BAT approaches, and inconsistent regulation on alternative technologies deters beneficial innovation. For example, one way to eliminate refrigerator cooling agents suspected of damaging the ozone layer involves replacing them with small amounts of propane and butane. But narrowly conceived safety regulations covering these gases seem to have impeded development of the new technology in the United States, while several leading European companies are already marketing the new products.

Develop regulations in sync with other countries or slightly ahead of them. It is important to minimize possible competitive disadvantages relative to foreign companies that are not yet subject to the same standard. Developing regulations slightly ahead of other countries will also maximize export potential in the pollution-control sector by raising incentives for innovation. When standards in the United States lead world developments, domestic companies get opportunities for valuable early-mover advantages. However, if standards are too far ahead or too different in character from those that are likely to apply to foreign competitors, industry may innovate in the wrong directions.

Make the regulatory process more stable and predictable. The regulatory process is as important as the standards. If standards and phase-in periods are set and accepted early enough and if regulators commit to keeping standards in place for, say, five years, industry can lock in and tackle root-cause solutions instead of hedging against the next twist or turn in government philosophy.

Require industry participation in setting standards from the beginning. U.S. regulation differs sharply from

European in its adversarial approach. Industry should help in designing phase-in periods, the content of regulations, and the most effective regulatory process. A predetermined set of information requests and interactions with industry representatives should be a mandatory part of the regulatory process. Both industry and regulators must work toward a climate of trust because industry needs to provide genuinely useful information and regulators need to take industry input seriously.

Develop strong technical capabilities among regulators. Regulators must understand an industry's economics and what drives its competitiveness. Better information exchange will help avoid costly gaming in which ill-informed companies use an array of lawyers and consultants to try to stall the poorly designed regulations of ill-informed regulators.

Minimize the time and resources consumed in the regulatory process itself. Time delays in granting permits are usually costly for companies. Self-regulation with periodic inspections would be more efficient than requiring formal approvals. Potential and actual litigation creates uncertainty and consumes resources. Mandatory arbitration procedures or rigid arbitration steps before litigation would lower costs and encourage innovation.

For an extended discussion of the ways in which environmental regulation should change, see Michael E. Porter and Claas van der Linde, "Toward a New Conception of the Environment-Competitiveness Relationship," Journal of Economic Perspectives 9, no. 4 (Fall 1995).

The New Environmentalists

ENVIRONMENTALISTS CAN FOSTER innovation and resource productivity by speaking out for the right kind of regulatory standards and by educating the public to demand innovative environmental solutions. The German section of Greenpeace, for example, noted in 1992 that a mixture of propane and butane was safer for cooling refrigerators than the then-prevalent cooling agents—hydrofluorocarbons or hydrochlorofluorocarbons—that were proposed as replacements for chlorofluorocarbons. Greenpeace for the first time in its history began endorsing a commercial product. It actually ran an advertising campaign for a refrigerator designed by Foron, a small refrigerator maker on the verge of bankruptcy. The action was greatly leveraged by extensive media coverage and has been a major reason behind the ensuing demand for Foron-built propane-butane refrigerators and the switch that the established refrigerator producers in Germany later made to the same technology.

Environmental organizations can support industry by becoming sources of information about best practices that may not be well known outside of a few pioneering companies. When it realized that German magazine publishers and readers alike were unaware of the much improved quality of chlorine-free paper, Greenpeace Germany issued a magazine printed on chlorine-free paper. It closely resembled the leading German political weekly, *Der Spiegel,* and it encouraged readers to demand that publishers switch to chlorine-free paper. Shortly after, *Der Spiegel* and several other large magazines did indeed switch. Other environmental organizations could shift some resources away from litigation to focus instead on funding and disseminating research on innovations that address environmental problems.

Among U.S. environmental groups, the Environmental Defense Fund (EDF) has been an innovator in its willingness to promote market-based regulatory systems and to work directly with industry. It supported the sulfur-dioxide trading system that allows companies either to reduce their own emissions or to buy emissions allowances from companies that have managed to exceed their reduction quotas at lower cost. The EDF-McDonald's Waste Reduction Task Force, formed in 1990, led to a substantial redesign of McDonald's packaging, including the elimination of the polystyrene-foam clamshell. EDF is now working with General Motors on plans to remove heavily polluting cars from the road and with Johnson & Johnson, McDonald's, NationsBank, The Prudential Insurance Company of America, Time Warner, and Duke University to promote the use of recycled paper.

Source: Benjamin C. Bonifant and Ian Ratcliffe, "Competitive Implications of Environmental Regulation in the Pulp and Paper Industry," working paper, Management Institute for Environment and Business, Washington, D.C., 1994.

Notes

1. One of the pioneering efforts to see environmental improvement this way is Joel Makower's *The E-Factor: The Bottom-Line Approach to Environmentally Responsible Business* (New York: Times Books, 1993).

2. Andrew King, "Improved Manufacturing Resulting from Learning from Waste: Causes, Importance, and Enabling Conditions," working paper, Stern School of Business, New York University, New York, 1994.

3. Mark H. Dorfman, Warren R. Muir, and Catherine G. Miller, *Environmental Dividends: Cutting More Chemical Wastes* (New York: INFORM, 1992).

4. Don L. Boroughs and Betsy Carpenter, "Helping the Planet and the Economy," *U.S. News and World Report* 110, no. 11, March 25, 1991, p. 46.

5. John H. Sheridan, "Attacking Wastes and Saving Money...
Some of the Time," *Industry Week,* February 17, 1992, p. 43.

6. Gerald Parkinson, "Reducing Wastes Can Be Cost-
Effective," *Chemical Engineering* 97, no. 7, July 1990, p. 30.

7. Stephen J. DeCanio, "Why Do Profitable Energy-Saving
Projects Languish?" working paper, Second International
Research Conference of the Greening of Industry Network,
Cambridge, Massachusetts, 1993.

8. Jan Paul Acton and Lloyd S. Dixon, "Superfund and Trans-
action Costs: The Experiences of Insurers and Very Large
Industrial Firms," working paper, Rand Institute for Civil
Justice, Santa Monica, California, 1992.

9. Norman Bonson, Neil McCubbin, and John B. Sprague,
"Kraft Mill Effluents in Ontario," report prepared for the
Technical Advisory Committee, Pulp and Paper Sector of
MISA, Ontario Ministry of the Environment, Toronto,
March 29, 1988, p. 166.

10. Parkinson, p. 30.

Originally published in September–October 1995
Reprint 95507

*The authors are grateful to Benjamin C. Bonifant, Daniel C. Esty, Donald
B. Marron, Jan Rivkin, Nicolaj Siggelkow, and R. David Simpson for
their extremely helpful comments; to the Management Institute for Environment and Business for joint research; and to Reed Hundt for ongoing
discussions that have greatly benefited the thinking behind this article.*

Recycling for Profit

The New Green Business Frontier

DAVID BIDDLE

Executive Summary

ALTHOUGH MODERN URBAN recycling programs have successfully created a tremendous supply of recycled newspapers, glass bottles, and office paper, when it comes to consumer and business demand for products made from these materials, the economics of recycling falls apart. As David Biddle notes, the present cost of collecting and processing recyclable materials far outweighs their value as a commodity that can be sold back to industry. Yet precisely because of this market uncertainty, companies can seize the competitive high ground.

Farsighted players have already found profitable openings. There's clearly consumer demand for green products, and Rubbermaid, Moore Business Forms, International Paper, and others have dramatically increased market share with appropriate offerings. In addition, top managers of companies like Bell Atlantic and Coca-Cola have made buying recycled products and investing in green R&D part of their business strategies. Through such efforts, business leaders help to challenge current recycling myths, including the supposed high price and low quality of recycled products.

While public policymakers are still trying to assess what's wrong with recycling programs, corporations are in the best position to take the lead. More important, given the potential profits to be made *and* the tighter government regulations that are sure to come, it's in their economic self-interest to do so. The Buy Recycled Business Alliance, which includes Bank of America, American Airlines, and Anheuser-Busch on its steering committee, indicates how profits and social responsibility may come together in the 1990s.

D ESPITE THE PROLIFERATION OF curbside collection bins and public awareness campaigns, recycling programs around the United States aren't working. Modern urban recycling, which began with the passage of New Jersey's mandatory recycling law in 1984, has successfully created a tremendous supply of recycled newspapers, glass bottles, office paper, and other materials. But when it comes to consumer and business demand for the products made from these materials, the economics of recycling falls apart. According to the press and other pundits, "recycling is a victim of its own success."

In fact, recycling is not just a matter of recovering recyclable material; it's a total economic system. Few people realize that their local curbside collection program is only the beginning of a recycling loop. At present, the cost of collecting and processing recyclable materials far outweighs their value as a commodity that can be sold back to industry. Unless consumers buy recycled products, the markets for the material they put out at the curb or into their office white-paper bin will remain depressed.

However, precisely because of this market uncertainty, companies can turn building demand for recycled products into a competitive advantage. In the 1990s, those companies that act quickly will exploit new product niches and manufacturing technologies. Farsighted players have already found profitable openings. There's clearly consumer demand for green products, and Rubbermaid, Moore Business Forms, and International Paper, to name but a few, have dramatically increased

Managers of American Airlines and Coca-Cola have made buying recycled products part of their overall business strategies.

market share with appropriate offerings. These companies have also anticipated the tighter environmental regulations that are sure to come. Rather than simply fighting government and community groups, corporations can now form strategic alliances with public organizations and other business interests.

While public policymakers are still trying to assess what's wrong with recycling programs, large corporations and small entrepreneurs alike are in the best position to take the lead. More important, it's in their economic interest to do so. Certainly, U.S. corporations shouldn't start running local collection programs or taking government's place in implementing policies that encompass many communities or an entire state. But business leaders can challenge current recycling myths, including the supposed high price and low quality of products. Top managers of companies like American Airlines, Bell Atlantic, and Coca-Cola have made buying recycled products and investing in green R&D part of their overall business strategies. They've cut down on waste, increased profit margins, and, in some cases, truly closed the recycling loop.

The success of recycling—indeed, its true value in the long term–won't depend on how much landfill space is saved but on whether or not recycling makes economic sense. To build demand for recycled materials, government and business must not only reinvent themselves, they must also reinvent their relationship, especially when it comes to economic problems that neither can solve alone.

Building Demand: The Recycling Markets Problem

The most common reason given for the current economic crisis in recycling is the supply and demand problem. Media stories abound about recycling centers and waste haulers dumping loads of plastic bottles, newspapers, or phone books into landfills after preparing them for markets that don't exist. The centers store them until they become unsightly mountains of "junk" and public health problems. True, this has occurred in some cases. But the real reason that recyclables often sit in recycling yards is that recyclers, like any good commodities brokers, "bet on the come." Mountains of recyclable material remain in storage while recyclers wait for the price to rise to a level that allows them to cover the cost of collection, transportation, processing, packaging, and storage—and to make a reasonable profit. (See "The High Cost of Processing What's Put Out at the Curb" at the end of this article.)

It's been an industrial buyer's market over the last several years for all recyclable commodities. End users of recycled raw material, or *feedstock*, can choose whom they wish to do business with and can assure that the price of the material they require will stay down. In many cases, recycled commodities must also compete with virgin raw materials. During the past two years, for example, the high-density polyethylene (HDPE) industry has developed an overcapacity of virgin resins.[1] The market is so flooded with "clean" material that the price for recovered forms of this plastic from curbside recycling programs has plummeted.

Recycled commodities often end up competing against one another as well. Nowhere is this more obvious than in the paper industry. With intensive recycling taking place in most major urban centers around the United States, the huge swell of *postconsumer* paper (recovered from curbside and office recycling programs) available to manufacturers of corrugated cardboard, newsprint, and toilet tissue allows them to play one material off another. A Pennsylvania manufacturer recently discontinued use of recycled newspaper in its production process because it negotiated a better price for recovered phone books. Office paper can be used to make high-grade stationery, but it's fast becoming one of the major feedstocks for lower grade paperboard and toilet tissue. That means recyclers must now pay higher prices to get rid of the low-grade, mixed junk paper that used to be one of their mainstays.

In the global marketplace, competition for recovered material exports is also intense. Asian countries, long a predictable export market for U.S. recycled-paper brokers, are opting to use European paper sources where the material is typically less contaminated and cheaper to transport. U.S. paper exports from 1991 to 1992 dropped by 6.4-million tons (2.3%) for the first time in decades, and the market value of exports fell by 7.9%. As the European waste-management infrastructure becomes increasingly sophisticated, U.S. suppliers have fallen farther behind in 1993.

For example, Germany's latest package-reduction ordinance requires that retailers take back all sales packaging from customers and add a 30-cent deposit to most nonrefillable containers. German manufacturers and product suppliers now pay a licensing fee to place a green dot on products; the green dot guarantees that a product's packaging will be recycled by the recycling industry. Since many German retailers now refuse to stock products without the dot, it's likely that 80% of all retail packaging will be recycled or eliminated by 1994.

Of course, some companies in other European Community countries have called these German initiatives protectionist. Antitrust suits, which claim that the green-dot program and other German restrictions necessitate agreements between competing companies in order to handle packaging waste, are still pending. Nevertheless, without the stimulus of such sweeping environmental regulations, most U.S. manufacturers during the 1980s didn't invest in the new plant technologies that now make German and other European companies much more competitive when it comes to waste management.

But U.S. manufacturers haven't always been so slow to invest. For decades, the steel and aluminum industries have successfully developed their respective technologies to incorporate large quantities of postconsumer recycled materials. Aluminum cans all contain a high percentage of recycled content, and virtually all products made with steel contain at least 25% reclaimed steel. The value of steel and aluminum to industry consistently guarantees that they are worthwhile components of curbside recycling programs. While steel and aluminum containers compete against each other as food and beverage packaging, each is a comparably low-cost, functional item that's embraced by consumers. In general, these two industries couldn't survive without the heavy input of recycled material; and in this, they are models for the lagging paper and plastics industries.

Strong demand for recycled products ultimately requires that these products, as in the case of steel and aluminum, be cost competitive and of high quality. It also requires that they be available in large enough quantities to allow for economies of scale. By mandating recycling and setting extremely high recovery goals for both

Steering-committee members of the Buy Recycled Business Alliance accounted for $3 billion in purchases of recyclables.

paper and plastics, government has challenged U.S. industry to develop the necessary infrastructure for incorporating these materials into manufacturing processes.[2] Yet for this challenge to be met, government and industry need to reach an understanding about the complexity of the problem that they are both attempting to tackle.

This understanding can only be established by developing a unified and coordinated approach. In Germany, the green-dot program funds the Duales System

Deutschland (DSD), known as the "dual system" because it works in tandem with an existing system of government recycling programs. The DSD is essentially a national recycling company formed by Germany's retailers and more than 600 product suppliers and distributors. Given the complications of negotiating business initiatives in the EC, the German model isn't strictly applicable to the United States; but it may offer U.S. companies lessons in the value of taking a proactive stance toward environmental issues and in the need to form public-private alliances.

Building demand for U.S. recyclables is a case in point. From a public-policy perspective, the recycling issues of collection and processing certainly require further technology and systems refinement. Over time, however, these costs are sure to come down. It's in stimulating the recycling markets that current policy—and business practice—will make the most difference. In the past two years alone, a number of national and local organizations and government groups have initiated "Buy Recycled" campaigns that actively encourage government agencies, businesses, nonprofits, and institutional organizations like hospitals to buy products made of recycled materials.

The Buy Recycled Business Alliance, for example, includes Bank of America, American Airlines, Bell Atlantic, Coca-Cola, and Anheuser-Busch on its steering committee of 33 companies. (See "Buy Recycled Business Alliance: 1993 Members" at the end of this article.) In less than one year, the steering-committee members alone have accounted for $3 billion in purchases of recycled-content products and material. Approximately 10% of this investment has been for internal purchases (such as office supplies and packaging) and 90% for external materials (raw feedstock like recovered paper, bottles, cans, and products for sale to the general public). By the end of 1995, the business alliance hopes to sign 5,000 companies as members.

Plenty of U.S. companies, of course, have already jumped on the green bandwagon. They've entered the market so hastily that the recycling symbol manufacturers put on products (the "chasing arrows") is now used indiscriminately. Sometimes the symbol means the product contains recycled materials; in other cases, it means the product itself is recyclable. As a result, today's consumers are both wary and confused about competing green claims. Although it's been easy enough for companies to take advantage of demand for high-quality green toilet tissue and paper towels (sold at relatively high prices), customers aren't so eager to buy or aren't even aware of the many other recycled products on the market.

It's in exposing misperceptions about the quality and "environmental correctness" of certain products (especially those made from plastic) that companies have the largest role to play. For many managers, the changes start by instituting new corporate purchasing policies, not by creating yet another green product that confuses consumers. Top-level managers in the Buy Recycled Business Alliance certainly recognize the need to take a consistent stance toward environmentally responsible products and to provide customers with the right information. However, while they believe in being good corporate citizens, they also see the possibilities for gaining market share as well as a loyal customer base.

Managers of New Jersey-based Marcal Paper Mills, for instance, believe that they have developed a loyal following of customers because of a marketing strategy that focuses on community recycling programs rather than private-sector processing facilities. In more than 1,000 northeastern U.S. communities with office-paper collection programs, Marcal accepts wastepaper for use in its manufacturing process. In exchange, each community includes at least one retail outlet that stocks Marcal paper products. Based on Marcal's experience, building demand for recycled products can be a powerful tool for building customer loyalty.

Buying Recycled Products: Three Myths

In promoting the purchase of recyclables, the recent efforts of private companies and public interest groups deliberately challenge several recycling myths. These myths linger because of the rocky history of recycled products and continue to stymie strong, positive growth for today's recycled-product industries. The three most prevalent misconceptions are that recycled products cost more, are of inferior quality, and aren't available in enough quantity even if you want to buy them. But the corporate examples detailed below illustrate how, contrary to myth, companies can gain a competitive leg up by investing in recycled product lines.

MYTH 1: RECYCLED PRODUCTS COST TOO MUCH

The most common reason purchasing managers give for not buying recycled products is that they're too expensive. However, most companies that are committed to the principles of recycling and waste reduction haven't paid higher prices just to support the public interest. Rather, they've instituted new procurement policies that offer additional business benefits. The computer division of American Airlines, for instance, has saved over

$100,000 by converting to 100% recycled paper. Printing
its annual report on recycled paper has saved American
another $33,000. These savings were achieved by making
the company's needs known to vendors and demanding
competitive prices.

The recycled paper that Moore Business Forms buys
to produce its products is no different in cost than nonrecycled paper. Like other big manufacturers, Moore—
which with more than 30% of the market is the largest
single producer of business forms in the world—has
guaranteed its paper supplier that the company will buy
a specific volume of paper on an annual basis. The difference between Moore and many of its competitors is that
the company's supplier makes recycled stock. This partnership allows both companies to make a profit on the
use and production of recyclables. Indeed, the commitment of Moore's president and chief operating officer,
John Anderluh, to environmentally responsible products
has allowed the company to expand its customer base.
Moore's ReGenesis paper has been its fastest growing
product line since the company began offering it in 1990.
The success of ReGenesis is due in part to Moore's bonus
system, which gives an additional 2% to 3% in sales commission to reps who sell recycled products.

In order to build such profitable partnerships, suppliers and distributors must be able to guarantee not only
competitive prices but also volume of sales over time.
Strategic partnerships that increase the length of contracts can often be used to negotiate lower prices on
recycled materials. In most cases, suppliers are willing to
guarantee competitive prices on recycled products for a
short term, say two years, if they're allowed to renegoti-
ate the next two years of pricing. And some suppliers
consider their recycled stock to be a loss leader: it can be

worth offering at a low price, provided business customers also negotiate contracts for products with better profit margins, such as letterhead or fine writing paper.

Just five years ago, it was nearly impossible to find a printer who carried recycled paper, let alone one who could give a good price for printing on recycled paper. Purchasing managers often found that they had to buy an entire pallet load of paper; otherwise, they'd have to pay a premium for breaking a pallet load purchased by the printer. But numerous small and large companies that shop around today will find that printers can now provide letterhead, business cards, and envelopes on recycled paper at the same price as virgin stock paper. This change in pricing has been brought about partly by business customers that have forced printers to compete and partly by manufacturers that have offered better prices to their customers.

Recycled products like paper and carpets are now cheaper than their virgin counterparts.

For example, by the end of 1993, the Hammermill Paper division of International Paper will be producing its line of 100% recycled copier-quality paper. This new product, called Unity DP, will have a lower brightness factor than standard bright white copier paper; but for most day-to-day office purposes, it's more than adequate. Hammermill is building a $100-million deinking plant in central Pennsylvania that will use only old newspaper and glossy magazines to make pulp for Unity DP. The goal: to compete with prices and quality that are the equivalent of virgin stock paper.

In addition to paper, there are a number of other products that have become less costly than their virgin counterparts. For instance, Image Carpets makes both industrial and residential carpets out of 2-liter plastic soda bottles and sells them for less than most other carpets. And for companies with large vehicle fleets, buying recapped tires can create real savings. In Pennsylvania, the Department of Transportation saved more than $250,000 in one transportation district by fitting the drive wheels of crew cabs and construction vehicles with recapped tires. In addition, with the cost of lumber rising dramatically over the past year—and with some help from growing economies of scale—Eberhard-Faber's new EcoWriter pencil, made of recycled cardboard and newsprint, is now the same basic price as the equivalent wood pencil.

MYTH 2: THE QUALITY OF RECYCLED PRODUCTS IS BAD

Though once a serious concern, quality control is no longer an issue when considering recycled products. Office machinery experts now acknowledge that recycled-content paper performs better in modern copiers and laser printers because of improved conditioning of the paper fibers as well as better adjustment to humidity and temperature conditions. In addition, many people who use recycled paper report that the reduced glare is less taxing on their eyes. As Eleanor Lewis, director of Ralph Nader's Government Purchasing Project, has said, "Paper does not have to be a light bulb that glows in the dark."

However, quality also involves aesthetic definitions of products, a factor difficult to quantify and impossible to keep constant. Aesthetic misperceptions still greatly influence purchasing decisions. Consider plastic lumber. True, it can cost up to four times as much as its wood counterpart, but it also doesn't rot, splinter, or break.

Plastic lumber picnic tables, benches, sheds, waste receptacles, retaining walls, and fences have all demonstrated immense savings over time due to low maintenance costs. Still, while plastic lumber represents a tremendous investment by the plastics industry and one of the best product applications for recycled plastics, the market has started to grow in only the last two years.

Although manufacturers have taken great pains to make their product look like wood, plastic lumber is still *not* wood. Both individual consumers and company purchasing managers think of wood as the material of choice because they are accustomed to it. In addition, wood has traditionally been associated with high quality. And in a corporate setting, the buyer of wood products and materials is usually not the person responsible for maintenance and repair. Phoenix Recycled Plastics, a Pennsylvania-based company, finds that the specifications it receives from purchasers often break project cost proposals into two separate categories: lumber in one category and paint and labor in the other. Yet its plastic lumber, one of the company's main product offerings, comes in a number of colors and doesn't require painting. Most of Phoenix Recycled Plastics's customers are clearly interested in recycled products; but they have trouble evaluating the available products because of their aesthetic preference for wood.

Plastic lumber has forced managers to weigh their aesthetic principles against practicality.

Indeed, plastic lumber has forced the issue of life-cycle cost considerations in purchasing. To a certain extent, it has forced managers to weigh their aesthetic principles against practicality. Overcoming these barriers takes time. In many cases, it also takes a manage-

ment directive to place the principle of positive environmental ethics on equal footing with the aesthetics of
wood or of office products made from other materials.
Ted Reed, president of The Data Group, decided that his
marketing research company should buy Hammermill's
Unity DP when he heard that it jammed less in copiers.
But while employees like the idea of using a paper made
with old newspapers and magazines, some won't send
reports to clients on off-white Unity DP. Reed plans to
include a description of the paper's contents on each
sheet in order to turn a potential perception problem—
"this company is unprofessional because it uses poor-
quality paper"—into a marketing plus—"this company is
environmentally responsible because it uses recycled
paper."

In general, the durability and consistency of today's
recycled products are far superior to those on the market
just three years ago. Quality control tests that were run
on products from 1990 and 1991 have little bearing on
products currently on the market. Consider the case of
remanufactured toner cartridges. In the late 1980s,
remanufacturers simply opened up old cartridges and
repacked them with new toner. Now they strip down cartridges and refit them with long-lasting, high-quality
drums and other components manufactured specifically
to allow a toner to be recharged eight to ten times.
Remanufacturers offer free servicing of laser printers as
part of their standard contracts, and responsible companies promise to repair at their own cost any printer that
malfunctions due to a faulty cartridge.

The increasingly good quality of recycled products
points to another difficult issue. While restriction of
trade is essentially illegal, recycled products, like any
product substitute, call into question established

markets. Some copier companies and a few laser-printer manufacturers won't honor service contracts or warranties if anything other than specified components and materials are used. Such restrictive contracts can also be found for car parts, computers, telecommunications equipment, and many other high-tech products and services. In addition, franchises and authorized service companies will sometimes use the name of the manufacturer as a front for their own restrictions. Where necessary, buyers and purchasing managers should force competition on service contracts and demand that manufacturers put into writing any restrictions on the use of their products.

MYTH 3: RECYCLED PRODUCTS AREN'T AVAILABLE WHEN YOU NEED THEM

The availability of recycled products was a real problem just a few years ago and still is when certain businesses, particularly publishers, require large amounts of materials to meet a hard deadline. But most standard business products are readily available today. Major writing-paper companies like James River now carry numerous grades of quality paper stock in a variety of colors. And in 1988, Rubbermaid, long a leader in janitorial products, started using recycled plastics in the production of recycling containers for New York City's curbside programs. Based on this early success in New York, the company saw the market potential for developing recycled versions of a number of its plastic products, including trash cans, buckets, liners, and wheeled carts.

Consumers Union identified opportunities for producing many of its publications with recycled paper.

Rubbermaid currently markets more than 70 products made from postconsumer plastic.

Even in the case of newspaper and magazine publishers that require large quantities of recycled paper in a short time, planning and vigilance can overcome the availability problem. For example, Consumers Union, which publishes *Consumer Reports*, examined the feasibility of converting the paper its magazine was printed on to recycled content. The driving force behind the use of recycled paper was Rhoda H. Karpatkin, Consumers Union's executive director. She believed that it was essential for her nonprofit organization to be sensitive to environmental considerations in its purchasing and publishing activities.

With a circulation of over five million, *Consumer Reports* is the eighth largest magazine in the United States. Initially, the magazine's typical publication run was too large to be accommodated by suppliers of recycled paper. However, Karpatkin and others persisted in their efforts. They identified opportunities for producing many of Consumers Union's other publications with recycled paper, including the *1992 Guide to Income Tax Preparation*. Over time, the magazine's suppliers were able to provide CR with paper that had varying degrees of recycled content for some of its issues at a nominally higher cost.

To compensate for the higher price, CR established a price preference fund that was partly fed by the savings from their in-house recycling program. Karpatkin and her staff also recognized that supporting the recycling industry's efforts in developing consistent materials would help it catch up to the magazine's needs. The recycled content of *Consumer Reports* continues to increase: half of the press run for *Consumer Reports* is now printed on recycled-content paper. In addition, more than half the books published by Consumers Union are currently printed on recycled paper. During the next several years, Consumers Union expects its suppliers to develop both a consistent feedstock and competitive prices.

To stave off potential legislation that would mandate recycled content in newsprint, the Pennsylvania Newspaper Publishers Association (PNPA) proposed a voluntary program that would increase its use of recycled-content newsprint to 50% by the year 1995. In 1988, PNPA found that recycled newsprint was at 8%. In 1993, the association estimates a level of 35%. PNPA is confident that the efforts of their 250 member papers can raise that level to 50% before the 1995 deadline. The only thing standing in PNPA's way is the availability of recycled newsprint—not the supply of old newspapers themselves but the blank sheets of newsprint produced by mills.

By the year 2000, every U.S. newspaper will contain at least some recycled content.

Ironically enough, while plenty of people dutifully bundle newspapers for recycling programs, a number of local recycling programs have stopped collecting them. While temporary, the glut in unprocessed newspapers highlights the problems caused by the time lag between collection and processing. Once again, it's not enough to stimulate supply *or* demand for a recycled commodity. In efficiently generating a supply of unprocessed newspaper, government programs have made a new resource available to industry. Manufacturers, in turn, are now scrambling to catch up by upgrading processes and creating new uses for recycled newspapers. By the year 2000, every U.S. newspaper will contain at least some recycled content.

A similar desire to outrun legislation moved Bell Atlantic Directory Services to research the use of recycled-content paper for its phone books. After extensive review of its options, the public utility learned that its only source of stock paper was a mill in Europe. At considerable investment to the company, the paper has been imported to the United States for use in publishing Bell Atlantic's phone books. The company has persisted in asking U.S. paper companies for directory stock paper at competitive prices. And in the next several years, a plant will probably be built in North America that can provide Bell Atlantic with all the paper it needs.

Investing in Green R&D: Strategic Alliances

Ten years ago, small U.S. companies and entrepreneurs were the ones investing in new manufacturing processes because they had the most to gain from entering niches for recycled products. However, as recently as the late 1980s, most large companies were still investing in plant upgrades for handling virgin natural resources. In order to produce recycled products of equivalent quality and price, then, industry must now invest heavily in new technologies. Socially responsible mission statements aside, R&D investment on this scale will occur for only two reasons: anticipated profits and the threat of competition.

In fact, a number of products have been made with recycled stock for decades, including steel and aluminum cans, soap, and low-cost toilet tissue. For the past 70 years, companies like Fort Howard, Wisconsin Tissue Mills, and Marcal have used wastepaper from mills and printers as the primary source of their manufacturing processes. By doing so, they tapped a cheap resource that allowed them to create tissue products for the low end of the market. At the same time, they didn't advertise the recycled-fiber content of their products because past consumers saw this as an indication of poor quality more than anything else. But with today's consumer demand for recycled-paper products, these companies have repackaged a number of their lines to present a greener face. And with the increasing supply of postconsumer wastepaper, especially from office recycling programs, all three have upgraded plants to handle this new feedstock. Now they're increasing market share by positioning themselves as companies that offer environmentally responsible products.

Or consider Rubbermaid, which has pioneered the use of postconsumer plastic in both blow-molding and injection-molding technologies, forcing smaller competitors like Zarn and Toter to follow suit. At present, the increased competition and the depressed market for postconsumer HDPE has chipped away at Rubbermaid's market share, particularly in trash cans and curbside recycling containers. But the company has responded by developing what they call a hands-on, closed-loop approach to feedstock acquisition, allowing better quality management of the recyclables they're using in the manufacturing process.

Because of Rubbermaid's closed-loop program, for example, it is now a leader in the recovery and reuse of low-density polyethylene (LDPE) stretch wrap. Using a small plastics-processing company to clean up the postconsumer LDPE, Rubbermaid buys stretch film from distribution centers for companies like Giant Foods. It ships them for processing and then buys converted pellets from the processor to use in the production of new products (such as recycling containers or trash cans) for resale to the same consumers. In order to close this loop

effectively—and profitably—Rubbermaid works with
both the processor and Giant Foods to ensure that the
plastics they recover for reuse are of the highest quality
and virtually free from contamination. Quality management is key, since it allows Rubbermaid to produce products in a number of attractive colors rather than the
usual black or gray containers made of recycled plastics.

Investing in green R&D creates many opportunities for
closing the recycling loop, from new manufacturing processes for a single product to a collection-and-processing
loop like Rubbermaid's. Although a number of large companies have started investing in new processes because of
competitive pressures, they've also developed strategic
alliances with public institutions, local government, or
other companies to help split the initial high costs of
R&D. In the case of International Paper, its Hammermill
division licensed the technology for producing Unity DP
from the German company Steinbeis Temming Papier.
For more than a decade, Steinbeis has been producing
Hammermill's Unity DP for the German market. Steinbeis
will continue to manufacture the paper for sale in the
United States until production at Hammermill's new
Pennsylvania plant is underway.

Of course, while Hammermill currently plans to price
Unity DP competitively in the United States, it had other
economic reasons for licensing the technology in 1990.
Since the licensing agreement with Steinbeis is exclusive,
it gives International Paper a niche in the growing market for environmentally responsible products. In addition, like most old-line industrial giants, International
Paper has had its share of environmental disasters.
Switching to more environmentally responsible processes will in and of itself help the company retain customers. Not to mention the fact that the wood-pulp

processing required to make virgin stock paper creates hazardous wastes that have become increasingly costly to clean up.

Coca-Cola's partnership with Hoechst Celanese exemplifies another strategic R&D alliance, in this case with a regular supplier. In addition to glass and aluminum recycling, Coca-Cola has invested in developing a 2-liter soda bottle made with 25% recycled post consumer plastic. Coca-Cola is committed to producing a range of environmentally responsible products; in particular, top managers wanted to address the public's negative attitude toward recycled plastics and the overall recyclability of plastics. Hoechst Celanese developed the new technology for Coca-Cola in order to remain the soft-drink giant's main supplier of plastic bottles. In exchange, Coca-Cola underwrote much of the R&D costs and allowed Hoechst to keep the rights to the technology.

The plastics that Coca-Cola uses to make its new bottle can be reused to make the same product, closing the recycling loop.

This new type of container has been accepted by the Food and Drug Administration for use in direct contact with beverages. The container's innovative packaging design closes the recycling loop, since the same plastics used in making the bottles can potentially be cycled back into Coca-Cola's manufacturing process and reused to make the same product. In order to gain approval for this new packaging technology, Coca-Cola had to convince the FDA that the company could handle any possibility of contamination or resulting health problems. As a result of this pioneering work by Coca-Cola and the FDA, some of the outdated government regulations for hygienic quality in the packaging of recyclables have been changed. Now other food and beverage containers made from postconsumer plastic—including jars and bottles for salad dressings, peanut butter, and ketchup—are either on the market or in development.

Bell Atlantic's approach to combining government and business interests presents an interesting twist on R&D costs. As a public utility, the phone company is subject to more government regulation than private companies, and, consequently, Bell has developed new manufacturing processes. Bell hasn't only invested in using recycled paper for its telephone directories, it has also extended resources into making the phone directories themselves recyclable. Among other things, Bell has eliminated the use of hot-melt binding glues that would literally gum up paper-pulp recycling operations. In addition, the company has done away with glossy paper covers.

However, Bell Atlantic and other utilities can also raise consumer rates to cover additional R&D expenses. This public-private balance of costs is delicate; but it can spur the larger changes a complicated economic issue like recycling requires. Bell has also invested heavily in establishing working phone-book recycling partnerships with local public-sector recycling programs in its service territory. Local recycling coordinators are responsible for setting up the collection and public-education component of the program, while Bell pays for transportation to markets and guarantees that recycled phone books will not be landfilled.

One of the best examples of a government-business partnership driven by leading-edge ingenuity can be found in Recycled Plastics Marketing of Seattle. RPM, a small but keenly entrepreneurial company, has entered into an agreement with the City of Seattle to produce a backyard composter for use in Seattle's intensive waste-reduction program. RPM's composter is made of 100%

recycled plastic. The program's inventiveness stems from the fact that the Seattle Composter is made of the HDPE milk jugs recovered in the city's recycling program. RPM receives a predictable flow of materials for its product, and the city guarantees payment on a large number of composters. The composters, in turn, are given to the city's residents for free; but their use reduces the quantity of trash that must be picked up at the curb, substantially cutting down on the city's waste-management costs. Cooperative partnerships like this demonstrate the potentially positive effects of recycling on local economic development—as well as how business and government can negotiate mutually beneficial deals.

Closing the Loop: The Business Case for Recycling

Some companies, of course, contribute to the public interest simply because they believe in the importance of doing so. For example, Conservatree Paper Company, a San Francisco–based recycled paper distributor, recently began a pilot project in 20 California school districts for the Inner-City School Donation Program. Under this program, Conservatree helps schools that have funding problems by donating paper supplies worth 1% of the company's total sales. Schools receive sorely needed supplies *and* recycled paper. From an educational standpoint, children get a chance to see the full recycling loop—from curbside collection to buying recycled products to recollection—in action.

But coordinating business-government programs to this extent is no easy task, whether a participating company is driven by public or private interest. Even in the case of the Seattle Composter, RPM and the city went back and forth with bids and counterbids for six months before the program was implemented. In many respects, the partnerships that do exist now, such as the Buy Recycled Business Alliance, are a public-private experiment in social change. Given that consumers currently receive mixed messages from industry, environmental groups, and their own local recycling programs—and given that recycling professionals still argue about everything from the value of bottle bills to whether or not there's a landfill crisis—how government and business achieve their respective recycling goals will doubtless shift and adapt over time.

In addition, business strategists and policymakers can't rely on hard data to model the benefits of recycling based on classic economic theory. Assuming that issues of feedstock supply, labeling standards, and pricing are adequately dealt with, whether full-scale demand for recycled products will actually create enough stability in the marketplace to assure the long-term economic viability of recycling infrastructure remains an open question. The Environmental Protection Agency's goal for the United States is to divert 40% of waste by the year 2000. That means individual consumers and companies would need to buy back approximately 80-million tons of recycled products per year. At present, 20-million tons of postconsumer material are purchased in the United States (about 50% by business) and turned back into recycled products.

Yet the simple economics of supply and demand can't fully capture the value of building demand for recyclables. When compared with their virgin counterparts, recycled products provide a number of intangible but increasingly crucial business benefits. From a marketing perspective, use of recycled office products or investment by industry in new technologies that use recycled feedstocks will help win new customers and retain old ones. In addition, reassessing procurement policies to determine if there are subtle prejudices against recycled products calls into question more general quality standards and buying practices that may cost more than management had assumed. Investment in recycled products also means more competition and will inevitably force design innovations and new technologies that can further lower production costs.

Needless to say, recycled products tend to be less energy intensive and often have a lower impact on the environment than their virgin counterparts. Although it's exceedingly difficult to calculate the relative levels of environmental and energy impact, it is conceivable that in the near future, U.S. companies and government agencies alike will list their investment in these products in an official green "report card." This report card (somewhat akin to the social balance sheets many German companies produce voluntarily) will detail the energy a company has saved and the pollution it has reduced through buying recycled products and developing new manufacturing technologies.

Even when it comes to policing industry claims for recycled content, business has the most to gain by helping to coordinate, rather than hindering, the efforts of the EPA, environmental groups, the Federal Trade Commission, and private companies. The Recycling Advisory Council to the EPA is making tremendous strides in working out suitable and acceptable standards for all parties. But since its technical capacity and understanding of recycled products increases yearly, industry is best equipped to lead the others. Witness Coca-Cola's efforts to change FDA regulations and testing procedures.

On a grander scale, consider the potential of recycling for revitalizing U.S. industry. With some of the cheapest power costs anywhere in the United States, the Pacific Northwest is a prime area for the paper industry to invest in plant retrofits that can use recycled feedstock instead of virgin wood pulp. In fact, a number of companies like Smurfit, International Paper, Georgia Pacific, and Weyerhaeuser have already done so.[3] Loggers can then be retrained to operate recycling vehicles, "mill" plastic lumber, operate paper balers, or work in deinking plants. Emphasizing the recycling industry just might be one answer to an ailing local economy, provided corporate managers and government policymakers are willing to work as partners rather than the usual adversaries.

The High Cost of Processing What's Put Out at the Curb

YES, THE SUPPLY OF available recycled material has increased dramatically over the past eight years. But, no, excess supply of material is not the only reason why current market prices remain depressed. Recycled products are less predictable and more subject to contamination than many of their virgin counterparts. And over the past 50 years, U.S. industry has developed technologies for assuring high-quality, low-contamination virgin raw materials as feedstock. The paper industry, in particular, has continually improved its processes for refining virgin feedstocks. The result: high-quality, low-cost sheets of nonrecycled paper.

The advent of modern recycling, of course, has created a large supply of a new potential feedstock, composed of recovered waste from curbside and office recycling programs. To satisfy the initial consumer demand for recycled paper, manufacturers retrofitted old, outmoded plants and tinkered with existing processes for virgin feedstock. Since the main paper-industry players had no guarantee that buyers would exist for predictable quantities of high-quality recycled feedstock, it made little sense for them to invest in completely new plants and processes. But the result of this tinkering, especially in the late 1970s and early 1980s, was paper that was both more expensive and of lower quality than competing virgin products.

Meanwhile, the scrap and recycling industry, with help from state and local governments, has set up intermediate processing centers or materials recovery facilities (MRFs) to deal with contamination problems. These facilities are often capital and labor intensive, with combined hand- and automated-sort systems for filtering materials into "cleaner" commodities. In theory, the end product should be relatively high-quality raw material that can be injected into existing industrial processes once reserved mostly for large-scale scrap dealers.

But for a variety of reasons, the cost of this processing step has been far greater than policymakers originally anticipated. A study by the National Solid Waste Management Association indicates that the average cost of processing curbside recyclables is approximately $50 per ton. The cost for newspaper is $20 to $55 per ton, while plastic milk jugs and soda bottles are in the range of $65 to $300 per ton.

With the average landfill tipping fee at less than $30 per ton nationwide, recycling is clearly an expensive proposition in the United States. On average, the total cost of collecting, transporting, and processing recyclable commodities is generally $150 to $200 per ton. By comparison, the average cost of collecting, transporting, processing, and disposing of trash is $100 to $125 per ton. The table below, "MRF Processing Costs and Material Prices," illustrates the relationship between processing costs and market prices. In general, aluminum is the only commodity processed by recycling programs that is clearly profitable.

Quite simply, prices paid for most of the materials processed at MRFs make it impossible to run a processing business without covering costs some other way. To get around this problem, MRF operators must charge local governments and waste haulers that collect recyclables for the service of assuring that recyclables are

MRF Processing Costs and Material Prices

Material	Average Processing Cost *(in dollars per ton)*	Market Price *(in dollars per ton)*
Newspaper	33.59	0–20
Cardboard	42.99	10–30
Mixed Paper	36.76	5–255
Aluminum Cans	143.41	500–600
Steel Cans	67.53	49–78
Clear Glass	72.76	50
Brown Glass	111.52	25–40
Green Glass	87.38	5–15
Mixed Glass	50.02	0
PET Plastic	183.84	40–200
HDPE Plastic	187.95	40–160
Paper (All Grades)	33.55	NA
Mixed Containers	83.36	NA
All Recyclables	50.30	NA

Source: *Solid Waste Management* newsletter, January 1993, University of Illinois at Chicago. Prices represent market quotes for the Midwest during the end of 1992.

indeed moved back into the industrial and manufacturing process. The other option? Operators discontinue servicing recyclables that lose money.

Buy Recycled Business Alliance: 1993 Members

Steering Committee:

American Airlines, Inc.
Anheuser-Busch, Inc.
AT&T Telephone & Telegraph Co.
Bank of America National Trust & Savings Assn.
Bell Atlantic Corp.
Browning-Ferris Industries, Inc.
The Coca-Cola Co.
Cracker Barrel Old Country Store, Inc.
E.I. DuPont de Nemours & Co.
Fort Howard Corp.
Garden State Paper Co., Inc.
James River Corp. of Virginia
Johnson & Johnson
Johnson Controls
Kmart Corp.
Laidlaw Inc.
Lever Brothers, Inc.
McDonald's Corp.
Menasha Corp.
Moore Business Forms, Inc.
Quaker Oats Co.
Quill Co., Inc.
Rock-Tenn Co.
Rubbermaid Inc.
Safeway Inc.

Sears, Roebuck and Co.
Wal-Mart, Inc.
Waste Management, Inc.
Wellman, Inc.
Wisconsin Tissue Mills

Associations:

American Plastics Council
Food Marketing Institute
Steel Can Recycling Institute

Notes

1. The Society for the Plastics Industry has assigned HDPE Code #1. HDPE is most commonly recovered in the form of one-gallon milk, water, and cider jugs.

2. Government recycling goals around the United States range from achieving a recycling rate of 25% to one as high as 60%. A recent study commissioned by the EPA indicates that Americans achieved a recycling rate of 17% in 1991.

3. According to the American Forest and Paper Association (a recent merger of the American Paper Institute, the National Forest Products Association, and the American Forest Council), over 100 U.S. paper mills are scheduled in the next three to five years to be retrofitted or rebuilt in order to handle the increasing demand for recycled-content products.

Originally Published in November–December 1993
Reprint 93601

The Case of the Environmental Impasse

ALISSA J. STERN

Executive Summary

EVEN IN AN INDUSTRY notorious for polluting rivers
and clear-cutting vast amounts of woodland, Vermilion
Paper Company long had a reputation for environmental
insensitivity. But in the mid-1980's, Vermilion began to
see the green writing on the wall. Peter Ostenson, director of offshore production, was one of a new generation
of managers partly responsible for this change in attitude. After selling Vermilion's skeptical CEO, Oliver Hibbing, on a strategy combining the business and environmental agendas, Ostenson set his sights on starting a
eucalyptus plantation in the country of Equitania.

Ostenson chose Wendell Buyck, a young and like-
minded manager, to head the effort. With little foreign
experience, Buyck had his work cut out for him, first in
gaining Equitanian government approval and then meeting the demands of provincial officials. But Buyck went

one unprecedented step further by calling a meeting with Equitanian environmentalists, who, after tense negotiations, agreed to take a position of "nondisapproval."

But six weeks later, a renegade Equitanian environmental group and a militant U.S. group launched a campaign to discredit Vermilion. An ad appearing in four U.S. newspapers accused the company of exploiting the Third World; later, the groups threatened to boycott Vermilion products if the company didn't halt its Equitanian project.

Vermilion's choices seemed stark. Ostenson argued that the company should stay and fight, but Hibbing wasn't interested: "Millions and millions of people haven't seen these ads. And if we write off this fairly small investment, they never will."

Four experts on business and the environment examine Vermilion's options and debate its next move.

ENVIRONMENTALISTS OF EVERY STRIPE disliked the Vermilion Paper Company. Even in an industry notorious for pumping rivers full of noxious waste and clear-cutting woodlands in county-sized chunks, Vermilion had a reputation for insensitivity. At one time or another, almost every jurisdiction in which it owned forests or mills had taken legal action against it for violating some environmental statute. In the 1970s, one of its own major stockholders sued the company for polluting a river the man liked to fish in.

Recently, however, Vermilion management had begun to see the green writing on the wall. The retirement of several executives who had begun their careers at a time when many people accepted pollution as a condition of progress had made way for fresh ideas and a more "socially responsible" manufacturing and marketing strategy. Moreover, consumers still associated the Vermilion name with good paper products at a good price and knew little or nothing of the company's shabby environmental record, so it was not too late to change course.

On the other hand, it was none too soon. Over the past five years, several international environmental groups had organized a campaign called Vermilion Action to inform the public about Vermilion's record and bring pressure to bear on the company to clean up its act. If environmentalists continued to target Vermilion as a public enemy, sooner or later the image would begin to stick.

In the mid-1980s, the company launched a campaign to change its image. Essentially a marketing effort, the campaign was built around the slogan "Green Vermilion" and consisted primarily of television ads and bright green labels on every bright red package of tissue and paper towels proclaiming environmentally friendly products and policies. For example, the company made much of the fact that it did not cut virgin forest, though in fact it had not cut any virgin forest in the United States since the mid-1940s, when it ran out of virgin forest to cut and went to tree farms. The green labels also declared in large type that the product inside was biodegradable, as if biodegradable paper were Vermilion's own scientific breakthrough. Still, the company actually did take steps to cut pollution at its paper mills even beyond state and federal air and water standards. It purchased the best new equipment and initiated research into new production methods that would reduce the amount of sulfites and chlorine used to make and bleach its paper.

So the new strategy was timely, disingenuous, and nevertheless real. Most executives cared more about the company's profits and image than about its environmental impact, but many saw the two as closely related and thought it ought to be possible to clean up operations enough to satisfy conscience and preserve Vermilion's good name in the marketplace without hurting dividends. There were even a few who believed that ways could be found to make paper profitably without polluting rivers or destroying ecologically valuable forests—and that it was the paper industry's responsibility to find them.

One of these was Peter Ostenson, director of offshore production, and it was offshore, especially in the Third World, that a genuine environmental policy would have its greatest impact. Vermilion expected its own pulp needs to grow some two million tons a year by the turn of the century, and tropical forests would inevitably provide much of the increase. The tropics were new to Vermilion, and Ostenson wanted to get off on the right foot. He was convinced that the environmental agenda and the business agenda had to come together to the benefit of both. Otherwise, they would collide to the detriment of both.

He had his work cut out for him selling this idea to top management. Oliver Hibbing, the president and CEO of Vermilion Paper, actively supported the so-called environmental strategy, but he made it clear to Ostenson that his first responsibility was to the stockholders.

"I'm a company man, Peter. So if you tell me we have to learn new ways of doing business because that's what our customers want, that's what we'll do. If I didn't buy that argument, I certainly wouldn't be spending all this money. But let somebody else run the environment. I'm with you on strategy—what more do you want?"

Ostenson always responded the same way. "It's a false distinction, Oliver. The company is *part* of the environment."

WITH RAIN FORESTS NEARLY as vast as those of Brazil or Indonesia, the nation of Equitania has a quarter of its 210 million acres of land in some type of forestry production. The country produces nearly 20% of the world's tropical hardwoods and supplies the wood for about two million tons of paper pulp annually. All told, forestry contributes some $2 billion annually in foreign exchange and is Equitania's second highest export earner. Japanese companies hold about half the foreign forestry concessions; the other half belongs to companies from South Korea, Malaysia, Thailand, Singapore, Hong Kong, and the Philippines.

In the mid-1980s, Vermilion Paper began exploring the possibility of starting a eucalyptus plantation in Equitania to help meet the company's growing pulp and paper needs. Ostenson and Hibbing calculated that by 1993, the venture would need to produce the raw material for about 500,000 tons of pulp per year at an estimated startup cost of roughly $350 million, plus $180 million for expansion of an existing pulp-and-paper mill in Indonesia to process Equitanian eucalyptus as it arrived by sea. On Ostenson's recommendation, they chose Wendell Buyck to set up an office in Palakra, the Equitanian capital, identify a site, and pursue Equitanian government approval.

Buyck had no foreign experience to speak of. What he did have, in addition to seven years' experience in Vermilion middle management and an undergraduate degree in forestry, was energy, intelligence, and determination.

Even more important, he shared Ostenson's views about incorporating sound environmental principles into Vermilion's business agenda.

On setting up shop in Palakra, Buyck found a bewildering array of government agencies and regulations. He quickly saw that many of the regulations were absurd and some of the agencies dishonest, but with little knowledge of the country and no capacity for bribery, he realized that all he could do was play by the rules.

An official at the Ministry of Forests encouraged him. "Many of us would rather deal with Americans because they try to comply with the law. Most Asian companies do not even make the attempt," he said. "On the other hand, that is probably why Americans do poorly here."

With this ambiguous advice to go on, Buyck decided to seek full, formal government authorization for the project at every step rather than run the risk of government sanctions at a later date. Although government authorization would not prevent officials from invoking additional regulations—or demanding payoffs—in the future, it would improve his odds of building a viable project.

As a first step, Buyck complied with foreign-investment regulations by forming a joint venture between Vermilion and Ankora Corporation, an Equitanian conglomerate dealing mostly in minerals and construction. As president of the joint venture, called Veranko, Buyck applied to the government for permission to create a eucalyptus plantation. In hopes that his application would move faster and more smoothly if he made friends and contacts at the ministries, Buyck met personally with dozens of key officials.

After months of delays, the government granted Veranko a 35-year, 398,000-acre concession in the Keewa

Tinang province. Almost half of the land had recently been lumbered for hardwoods, and the foreign timber company involved had leveled the forest. This clear-cutting was an asset for Veranko. Buyck's plan to farm eucalyptus required open land, and Buyck had been looking for a recently logged parcel, partly so Veranko wouldn't have to cut any rain forest, partly for the satis-faction of reclaiming—and being seen to reclaim—defor-ested, despoiled land.

Government permit in hand, Buyck then turned his attention to nongovernmental bodies with stakes in the forest industry. The most powerful of these was Equi-trass, the Equitanian Trade Association, a kind of self-appointed but quasi-official regulatory agency that enforced the rules of a dozen ministries—generously for member companies, harshly for others. While member-ship dues were modest, Equitrass also assessed large mandatory fees for its "production fund." Refusing to pay was tantamount to refusing to join, and refusing to join meant certain failure. Veranko chose to join and to make the production fund payments.

Buyck's next move was suggested by the experience of foreign companies in several nearby countries. In Indonesia, for example, the residents of one town ran-sacked and forced the closure of a Dutch-owned rubber plantation because the company had operated without community approval. In Malaysia, villagers revolted against logging in the rain forest even though the timber company had struck a deal with provincial leaders.

Suspecting that a concession from the government was not enough, Buyck decided that Veranko should seek approval directly from the local residents. Locating the plantation in Keewa Tinang increased the potential for problems because the Keewatinians resented the economic and political domination of the central government at Palakra, which they saw as little better than a colonialist power. They were also concerned about losing ultimate ownership rights to a foreign corporation and about the fate of their villages, lakes, and sacred tribal sites.

Buyck agreed to lease the land directly from the Keewatinians for a term of 35 years at a specified fee, in addition to the rent negotiated with the government in Palakra. He further assured local and provincial officials that he would keep the plantation away from villages, watersheds, lakes, and religious sites and that he would set aside the remaining rain forest in the concession as a nature preserve. Buyck also agreed to employ local people and to provide the province with a hospital, a school, and 100 kilometers of roads.

In Michigan, management was nervous. Hospitals, schools—was Buyck promising too much?

"He met our demands," recalls one community leader. "Other companies just come in and do whatever they want. Buyck was willing to listen."

Wendell Buyck had now spent nearly two years in Equitania. To Hibbing and the directors back in Michigan, progress seemed painfully slow. At this rate, the paper mill would come on line years behind the market opportunity. And now this man Buyck was agreeing to build schools and hospitals. Preserving virgin rain forest had the right sound to it, but schools and hospitals? Vermilion Paper was not a general contractor and certainly not a social service organization. These commitments might have some public relations value, but what about all those millions of paper towels that wouldn't be sold while Vermilion saved the world?

Peter Ostenson had to remind his superiors that Buyck was not trying to save the world, only Vermilion Paper. He took every opportunity to resell the environmental strategy to Hibbing, who still did not entirely buy Ostenson's contention that the time and money spent on this one project could pay a tenfold return in Third World goodwill, marketplace approval, and the increasingly well-publicized scorekeeping of environmentalists.

Ostenson reminded management that Buyck was only trying to save Vermilion, not the world.

Ostenson himself began to wish that Buyck could move faster. But Buyck could smell victory on his own terms and was making no compromises. His next move was to conduct a six-month pilot study in the concession area to find a fast-growing species of eucalyptus. Of 109 varieties, Buyck chose one that would permit harvesting every five years, instead of the usual six to eight, which meant Veranko could grow more trees in less space.

The pilot study impressed the Equitanian government. "We would be in great shape if all companies were as thorough as Vermilion Paper," one official at the Ministry of Forests told Buyck.

Finally, Buyck began to address the concerns of Equitanian environmental groups, an unprecedented step for any foreign corporation. He asked the leaders of PELLONA, a consortium of more than 100 Equitanian environmental and community groups, for their advice on the Veranko project. Initially, PELLONA was unwilling to talk to Buyck because it feared alienating its own constituency. At the time, PELLONA was aligned with the international Vermilion Action campaign.

"Buyck was different, or at least he sounded different," recalls Maria Biwapik, PELLONA's director. "But we found it hard to believe that Vermilion had really changed its stripes. In fact, Buyck was a little too good to be true. Because he worked for Vermilion, we drew the obvious conclusion: he *wasn't* true. He was just Vermilion's way of getting its hands on that concession. Once it co-opted all the potential opposition, it would revert to business as usual—cutting rain forest, draining wetlands, ignoring the natives."

Buyck was undaunted by PELLONA's refusal to listen. He turned to the minister of environmental affairs—by now a friend—and asked him to set up a discussion between Veranko and PELLONA. After much urging and arm-twisting, PELLONA finally agreed to a meeting, but only after an internal struggle between PELLONA leadership and a group of dissenting member organizations led by MYP, a small, militant organization that opposed all further forest exploitation in Equitania. Since a closed meeting with Buyck would conjure up the awful specter of PELLONA getting into bed with the enemy, the meeting was to include delegates from at least a dozen PELLONA constituents, MYP among them. No one in PELLONA was taking any chances. In a meeting with deforesters, there had to be witnesses, consensus, and daylight.

Buyck opened the meeting by reading a statement picturing Veranko as a friend of the environment, supporting the concept of environmentally responsible development, and asking for a common effort to make such a strategy work—in effect a quid pro quo between business and environmental interests. Hackles rose. The MYP representative attacked Vermilion at length. Buyck backpedaled.

He said he was sorry if he had offended anyone and told them he needed their help. He then spoke passion-

ately of his personal convictions. He told them how carefully and conscientiously he had satisfied the demands of
government ministries. He described his negotiations
with the tribal elders in Keewa Tinang, emphasizing the
school and hospital. He made much of the pilot project.
He underlined the fact that Veranko would plant only on
land already cleared and would cut no new rain forest.
He avoided any mention of resistance within his own
company.

He did not succeed in allaying suspicions—dislike of
Vermilion was too intense for that—but Maria Biwapik,
for one, began to sense an opportunity. If Buyck meant
even half of what he said, why not hold him to his word,
seize him by his outstretched hand, and not let go? And
why not use the opportunity to give PELLONA some
valuable limelight?

She asked Buyck if he would sign a binding agreement
limiting the size of the tree farm and guaranteeing the
rain forest now within the concession as a permanent
preserve. She also asked him to give PELLONA a permanent right of access and oversight. She rejected the idea
of a quid pro quo but pointed out that PELLONA could
hardly raise comprehensive objections to a plantation
operated according to a plan that PELLONA itself had
helped create and had the right to monitor.

Buyck blanched. He knew that Vermilion could not
possibly yield anything approaching even token control
of its operations to environmentalists, even if they had
been a lot more friendly than PELLONA. He proposed a
compromise. Veranko would hire PELLONA as a consultant to the project. He offered a fee of $20,000.

The MYP delegate called it blood money. Biwapik and
the others wanted to know what guarantee they had that
Veranko would follow their recommendations. "None,"

Buyck said. But what guarantee did they have now? He needed their advice, he said. His record demonstrated an honest desire to do right by the rain forest, by Equitania, and by the Keewatinians. He reminded them that he had asked for this meeting. He assured them that enlightened Vermilion leadership had come to believe—as this project made clear—that the paper industry could live in harmony with the environment.

It wasn't much, but it was more than Biwapik had expected. She actually found herself believing in Buyck's sincerity. The following day, the PELLONA steering committee held a long, heated meeting. No single delegate or member organization believed Vermilion could be trusted, but, like Biwapik, most instinctively trusted Buyck. Only the MYP delegate and one or two others held fast to the too-good-to-be-true theory and thought Buyck was actually lying.

"Nondisapproval" meant PELLONA wouldn't condemn Veranko—but would keep its options open.

In the end, the steering committee voted to accept the consulting assignment, refuse the fee, and take a position of guarded "nondisapproval" of the Veranko project. What that meant in practice, Maria later explained to Buyck on the phone, was that for the time being, PELLONA would refrain from condemning Veranko but would keep its options open. "That's all I ask," Buyck said. "But what about MYP?" Though she had her doubts, Maria assured him that MYP would consent.

In fact, MYP had voted loudly against any form of cooperation with Vermilion. But MYP was chronically short of money, and if it wanted to remain inside PELLONA and use PELLONA's resources, it would have to go along with the majority—or so Maria reasoned. Of course

MYP had a point: Vermilion certainly wasn't to be trusted and had to be watched closely. But this could be the chance PELLONA had been waiting for to bring pressure to bear on other foreign companies and convince the government and Equitrass that a strict environmental policy could work. And if PELLONA could take some of the credit for a success in Keewa Tinang, which Buyck's arrangement would let it do, so much the better. She wasn't about to let MYP sabotage such a rich opportunity.

For his part, Buyck was immensely pleased and relieved. He knew Hibbing was close to abandoning the whole project out of sheer impatience. Now Ostenson could tell him the project had passed its last great hurdle. Detailed planning and construction could now proceed with the blessings of the Equitanian government, the trade association, the Keewatinian community, and, however guardedly, some of the very environmental groups that had been supporting the Vermilion Action campaign. Reason had won a victory over both greed and passion. The environmental strategy was going to be a success. Buyck and Ostenson were vindicated.

Six weeks later, the Forest Defense Legion—a militant U.S. environmental group with close, informal ties to the Equitanian MYP—ran in four major U.S. dailies a full-page ad condemning Vermilion. (See "398,000 Acres of Virgin Rain Forest Down the Drain" at the end of this article.)

The Forest Defense Legion held a press conference later the same day to announce that unless Vermilion cancelled its project in Keewa Tinang within 30 days, the FDL would organize a worldwide boycott of Vermilion products.

The following day, meetings were held in Equitania and Michigan. In Equitania, Maria Biwapik and the other members of the PELLONA steering committee considered ways of limiting the damage. If Vermilion canceled the project, that was the end of PELLONA's golden opportunity to play in a bigger league and convert its convictions into practice. But if PELLONA defended Vermilion Paper and urged it to stay, it risked the utter loss of its credibility with other environmentalists.

Maria and many of the others were furious with MYP. "Why in God's name did you have to pick Vermilion?" she demanded. "There are a dozen worse companies doing business in this country and a thousand worse projects. What were you thinking of?"

"Don't climb on that high horse with me," the man from MYP responded angrily. "Are you trying to tell me that once our backs are turned, they won't cut rain forest to raise their yield? You're naive. They're all run for profit, these companies, and we attack them where we can. Most of the others have no retail customers we can appeal to. Vermilion does. It's as simple as that."

"I'm afraid you're the one who's naive," Maria said. "Please tell me what other company is even going to make the effort to work with us after this? Not only have you thrown away our chance to influence this project and every other forest project still to come, now we're going to have the government and Equitrass on our backs as well."

She paused. "This could set back the cause of the rain forest by ten years," she said. "And it could ruin PELLONA."

In Michigan, the choices were equally stark. Ostenson wanted to fight. The sheer injustice of the accusations made him dizzy. Who were these people? Did they really mean to make it impossible to change?

"If we don't fight this," he argued, "we lose not only the concession but also the strategy. Aside from the fact that it's so damned unfair, it's a business mistake to cut and run."

But Hibbing was not interested. "Peter, I don't know what you and Buyck think you've been up to these past three years, but it sure as hell hasn't been a business agenda. How is it *possible* you didn't see this coming? You weren't born yesterday. Buyck's been playing footsy with every bleeding heart in the Far East, and now the whole thing's exploded in his hands. What did he expect?"

"No one could have predicted that this one little group would go nuclear on us. Buyck made a superhuman effort to work with those people, and I still think he was right. We have to stand behind him and Veranko or give up the pretense of having any strategy or vision beyond our own bottom line. We're on trial here. Canceling is an admission of guilt—and we're not guilty."

Hibbing was icily patient. "Millions and millions of people haven't seen these ads," he said. "And if we write off this fairly small investment, they never will. If we fight it, we're inviting a worldwide boycott that will make Vermilion Action look pale by comparison. We're only on trial if we choose to be. Justice, Peter, has no net present value."

"Okay, you're right. This is not a question of justice," Ostenson said. "But it's not a question of image either. It's a question of strategy, tactics. To protect this company over the long haul, we simply can't lose sight of the bigger issues."

Hibbing gave Ostenson a long, cold look. "Well, then, how about this for a bigger issue. If we fight this thing, the stockholders would be fully justified in getting rid of both of us. And then having us committed. Boycotts are a kind of lunacy, Peter, and—maybe you're right—a kind of politics. But I'm a businessman. What are you?"

Should Vermilion fight or fold?

Four experts in environmental strategy discuss the options.

> PIETER WINSEMIUS *is director of the Amsterdam office of McKinsey & Company and leads its worldwide environmental practice. He was the Netherlands' minister of environment from 1982 to 1986.*

Much like individuals, organizations react to challenge in predictable ways. First comes denial of the problem; then anger; and finally, the search for a solution. Oliver Hibbing and Peter Ostenson should take heed. Even though Wendell Buyck would be justified in reacting this way, it would be counterproductive for him to do so. Vermilion executives may be hurt, but they must swallow their pride and refrain from calling "foul." They have to deal pragmatically with the problem at hand.

First and foremost, Ostenson must convince Hibbing to buy into his views on the environment. In doing so, Ostenson should abide by three principles.

Be responsive. Vermilion should organize a response that stresses accountability. Hibbing, as chief executive officer, should take responsibility for Vermilion's actions. He must be open with the press and the public; outsiders have an uncanny instinct for detecting half-truths or escapism. A straightforword response will demonstrate

that Vermilion takes the concerns of consumers and
environmentalists seriously.

Vermilion has a pretty good record in Equitania; why
not emphasize it? Hibbing could publicly offer, and con-
firmin large-scale advertisements, to conduct an environmental impact assessment—or even more appropri-
ately in this case, a societal impact assessment. Hibbing
can present this to PELLONA, the Forest Defense Legion,
or any other group for scrutiny. Most important, he can
eliminate many doubts with regard to self-serving sweet-
heart statements by asking a group of world-class
experts to give a second opinion, again publicly. Given
the amount of homework already done, this should be
relatively easy and should deflate much of the challenge
from the FDL and the MYP.

Learn from experience.   Clearly, Vermilion must review
its internal procedures and take measures to prevent
falling into this trap again. At the minimum, it should
reassess its own personnel policies. People in pivotal positions must have both the will and the skill to deal with
such crises. It is unfair and a waste of good resources to
send an inexperienced young talent like Buyck on such an
important and complicated mission. Considering the
mistakes he made—offering payment to environmental
groups for consulting services and trying to gain sympa-
thy by distancing himself from his company—I find it
amazing that Buyck survived as long as he did. Vermilion
would have fared far better if Buyck were backed by
strong nationals or, ideally, if Vermilion had educated
and trained Equitanians to run this project.

This points to a weakness often found among even
the largest multinationals: a lack of international management expertise amplified by an alarming degree of

environmental naivete. Many companies are shocked when they encounter protests from activists who rarely forgive environmental "mishaps," especially ones caused by "foreigners." Vermilion should form an advisory board of international outside experts who will meet several times a year and will help keep the company on its toes. Vermilion should also consider appointing someone with a strong environmental background to its board of directors.

Finally, Vermilion should launch a full-scale investigation of the safety and environmental risks of all activities at all sites. Though costly, this a doable exercise that provides a solid framework for creating action programs that reduce the risks associated with products, processes, and facilities. It enhances the organizational ability to deal with any remaining risks through environmental skill building, installing appropriate safety devices and information systems, and developing the expertise and procedures necessary for emergency management.

This operational assessment can be supported by an additional strategic focus attained through a policy impact assessment, which provides structured insight into the potential impact of new environmental policies in different countries. Contrary to popular belief, environmental policy tends to be quite predictable once one understands the underlying logic and the cultures of the players involved. By providing a window on the future, such an assessment can be a powerful tool in planning corporate strategic development.

Don't back down. Above all, Vermilion should not retreat from the progress it has made toward sounder environmental policy. As Peter Ostenson points out, that would be a business mistake. It would also send a negative signal to all Vermilion employees that could erode much of the environmental groundwork the company has laid in the last five years. And it would provide further "evidence" for the environmentalists' Vermilion Action campaign and would do little good for the company's own Green Vermilion campaign.

In the long run, Vermilion will need to find new sources for its pulp supply. Forest management in the Third World can benefit both the company and its host countries. The pulp and paper industry, with its vast consumption of natural resources and its highly visible presence in consumer products and household waste, must expect increasing environmental scrutiny from the public, from policymakers—even from employees, who want to be proud of the company they work for. The environment is no longer a side issue for only governments and environmentalists to worry about. No company can permit itself to live in disharmony with the environment.

ANTHONY L. ANDERSEN *is president and CEO of H.B. Fuller, a chemical products company headquartered in Saint Paul, Minnesota.*

Vermilion should move forward with its plans in Equitania. As a global company with a growing need for pulp from outside the United States, it should be committed to making this test case a success. If it can't find the pulp in Equitania, it will have to find it elsewhere. And no matter where it goes, it will find conditions like those in Equitania.

Moreover, Vermilion's bad reputation will precede it. The Forest Defense Legion will see to that. Vermilion's marketing campaign to convince the public of its environmental soundness didn't cut the mustard with anybody for one simple reason: you can't just talk about doing something; you have to do it—and do it well over time.

For these reasons, Vermilion should not undertake a campaign against the FDL. The company cannot outtalk the group. Instead, it should humbly and strongly build the coalitions it has already begun. Vermilion should recognize this not as a short-term event but as part of a long-term strategic plan: the company needs pulp today and will need it tomorrow. It should move forward with these seven steps.

1. Obtain an option to roll over the lease of the property beyond 35 years. Go for 50 years. Go for 70, 100. The whole purpose of concern for the environment is long-term existence and balance. If Vermilion doesn't send a clear message of long-term commitment, it is not being honest with shareholders, environmental groups, or governments.

2. Formalize the agreements with the federal government of Equitania and the provincial government of Keewa Tinang. Establish that the terms are for the full length of the lease—that there will be no changing the rules without mutual consent. This is not an inappropriate request: Weyerhauser and other paper companies that grow their own trees have 100-year plans for the use of resources.

3. Convince Oliver Hibbing to "make his stand." Hibbing is going to have to make a public stand on this issue or be booed out of office by investors or the board of directors. First, he needs to acknowledge that environmentalists have an important role to play in Vermilion's long-term strategy. Until he does this, the company will always be under pressure. Furthermore, Hibbing's involvement up front, both internally and externally, could make him a hero. He could come out of this positively received by all constituencies. In that sense, this confrontation represents an opportunity for Vermilion to make progress: dramatic situations call for dramatic actions. Hibbing must commit his full support or drop the whole initiative.

4. Encourage the FDL to meet with and join PELLONA. This will bring U. S. environmental groups into the process of monitoring Vermilion's operations in Equitania. This will also force the FDL to put up or shut up. It is going to be either part of the problem or part of the solution; this way, the FDL is part of the solution.

5. Hold off on any board decision until the MYP and FDL are part of the project. In other words, be vulnerable. Vermilion should open itself up and say that it won't make a decision until these groups are part of the process. Then if the MYP and FDL drag their feet, local governmental organizations will have a stake in this issue, will worry about the loss of jobs, and so might actually pressure the groups to join the project. Moreover, Vermilion directors should be given the time to visit, observe, and make an informed decision. I would schedule the board meeting at least six months in advance so that the board perceives a real opportunity to make the right decision.

6. Continue to build on the relationship with Maria Biwapik. Credit her publicly for anything positive that comes along, and make it clear that Vermilion genuinely appreciates her efforts. Biwapik is taking quite a risk, and risk takers have to be encouraged.

7. Take no action against the FDL for its newspaper ad. Let the attack go unchallenged—no retaliatory ads or lawsuits. Don't inflame the conflict in the media: that's an impossible battle to win. Play it cool and defuse the emotion. If Vermilion challenges the FDL's claims, its past will come back to haunt the company.

Vermilion will have to get along with the environmental groups for the length of the lease. If it starts the project in a confrontational way, some people might react emotionally and make it their objective never to give Vermilion any peace.

JACQUELINE ALOISI DE LARDEREL *is director of the industry and environment office at the United Nations Environment Program in Paris. The views expressed here do not necessarily represent the policy statement of UNEP.*

The public meltdown over the Equitanian project will force Vermilion to take at least one positive step: confront the fact that it has no overall environmental policy. Vermilion must stop reacting to external pressure on an ad hoc basis and begin to incorporate the environmental dimension in its long-term strategy. Until Vermilion does this, these crises will inevitably occur.

Vermilion's top management merely pays lip service to environmental concerns. Indeed, Oliver Hibbing's speeches show that the company does not value them at all. For all its hype, Vermilion has not incorporated environmental values into its decision-making process. It lacks even the most basic procedures or mechanisms to deal with environmental issues. It did not, for instance, subject the Veranko project to an environmental impact assessment—a tool that since the mid-1980s has been an effective way to assess potential environmental impacts and identify possible remedies. Nor does Vermilion value the ability to deal with environmental issues and related problems as a criterion in choosing its managers. The company provides no incentive to develop cleaner processes, while those who do take action—such as Wendell Buyck—are left without support.

Buyck's results are not as negative as they sound. He has initiated a successful dialogue with many of the partners, including the environmental groups. Yet despite his good and genuine intentions, Buyck was bound to fail without any true management support. He was unable to defend his statements picturing Vermilion as a friend of the environment because he had no credibility. He lacked the data to show both the environmental performance of Vermilion's operations in other parts of the world and the environmental impact of his project.

Buyck also failed because he doesn't have the proper skills and experience. He could have pushed the Equitrass negotiations as an opportunity to incorporate environmental principles into Vermilion's agenda. He never discussed a replantation or reforestation plan with the community, nor did he suggest organizing the training of local people in forestry. Finally, he contacted the environmental groups too late in the process.

Vermilion must start to follow through on its environmental claims. It cannot use marketing to address the environment—as it did when it launched an advertising campaign to tout the environmental investments it made only when activists began to apply pressure! As Sigvard Hoggren, a vice president of Volvo, has said, the most dangerous thing you can do is to look at your environmental ethics as a PR exercise: this won't work. The point is that it is the action that counts—not the hype. And not action merely in one plant but in the whole company. Vermilion needs to start thinking about the environment as an issue that won't go away. It needs to assess the environmental impact of the company's products, processes, and facilities. And it needs to translate its environmental values into practice—from training employees to deciding whether to use recycled or virgin pulp.

The Veranko joint venture should not be abandoned but be rethought in the framework of this new global policy. The Veranko case can be used to show Vermilion's willingness to change its policy. I would keep Buyck in the project: he has opened the dialogue, he has a good local image, and he believes in what he is doing. What he needs is backup. Vermilion should provide someone with experience who will help Buyck take advantage of the valuable work he has already done and the solid relationships he has already built. Above all, the company should continue the important dialogues Buyck has established—even with the Forest Defense Legion.

Vermilion should not shut down the project but continue moving forward at a slower pace. This is a long-term process that requires flexibility as the company learns how to implement its policy goals. The more immediate action Vermilion needs to take is the one it should have taken at the beginning of the process: to think through just how its overall environmental policy fits within its global company strategy and then design steps to make the policy work.

JAY D. HAIR *is president of the National Wildlife Federation, a private, nonprofit conservation organization based in Washington, D.C.*

Vermilion has no option but to press on with its plans. The cost of forgoing this venture goes far beyond a negative return on investment: Peter Ostenson and Wendell Buyck have provided a rare and valuable blueprint for other corporations to follow in developing environmentally sound business strategies. If this experiment fails, the corporate and environmental communities will both be worse off for it.

Vermilion's problem is one of trust. Its reputation is a result of years of insensitivity to environmental concerns and will not be easy to change. The environmental community has learned from dealing with Vermilion that caution, wariness, and a healthy dose of skepticism are good qualities to have. So how can Vermilion change its image and gain the acceptance and cooperation of environmental groups? There are four strategic steps the company can take to build on the trust established by Ostenson and Buyck.

Avoid quick fixes. Green cheerleading without substance invites a backlash that will negate whatever environmental goodwill a company has shown. For Vermilion and other companies, justice may have no net present value, but corporate greenwash promises an equally dismal rate of return.

Implement progressive environmental protection programs. Going above and beyond the call of regulatory duty is a sure way to gain the attention and respect of environmentalists. Companies will find them more willing to listen if environmental improvements are driven by culture rather than compliance.

Don't cut corners. Buyck's meticulous efforts to involve all interest groups in the planning and development process have been instrumental in his successes so far. Community involvement and respect for cultural diversity are essential for any development game plan.

Recognize the expanded role of corporations in achieving sustainable economic development. Environmental protection is the tip of the social policy iceberg. Buyck was right on target in trying to involve the company in local health and education improvement programs. Sustainable development involves more than just environmental protection. If Vermilion ignores other critical social needs, the whole development effort is in danger of collapsing.

Overall, Vermilion should avoid two mistaken conclusions from this experience. First, the company may be tempted to pursue a divide-and-conquer strategy and take advantage of what it perceives to be a fragmented environmental front. This would be disastrous. There is diversity within the environmental community, just as there is diversity in any industry trade group. But as every biologist knows, diversity is a sign of health, vitality, and strength. Environmental groups have proven their effectiveness in working together and make a formidable team. Corporations electing to manage their environmental affairs by playing interest groups off each other are destined to fail.

The other, equally erroneous conclusion would be that the effort was a waste of time and that an anticorporate bias will eventually doom any proactive measures Vermilion decides to pursue. The bottom line is that environmental groups do have responsibilities regarding their involvement with corporations. As environmental advocates, we have a responsibility to criticize companies that have been negligent in their environmental stewardship and to draw public attention to them. We also have an obligation to promote and support exemplary corporate environmental accomplishments. That means identifying positive actions a company may take to improve environmental quality and offering alternative solutions to problems when we believe the proposed options are not enough.

These principles are particularly relevant to Vermilion. The environmental community can be an important touchstone for industry in identifying issues of public concern and in establishing the trust and communication necessary for beneficial environmental practices. Nevertheless, there will always be some inherent conflict. Even if Vermilion sheds its old habits and follows a strategy of always "doing the right thing," it may face opposition from environmentalists in the future. Why? Because there will be occasions when the long-term ecological values at stake are so great that the best mitigation and contingency plans will not sufficiently address environmentalists' concerns.

Equitania, however, is not one of those situations. The clock is ticking. Oliver Hibbing should increase his visibility, take the offensive, and bring in the environmental, governmental, and public opinion leaders to participate in the development plan. He must demonstrate his personal and lasting commitment to Buyck's efforts. If the plan is as good as advertised, he will find a very receptive and helpful audience.

398,000 Acres of Virgin Rain Forest Down the Drain

IN THIS CENTURY, Vermilion Paper has clear-cut thousands of square miles of virgin forest in the United States and Canada. Now that our forests are gone, Vermilion is targeting the Third World.

In one of the most remote and unspoiled regions of Equitania, Vermilion Paper has acquired a concession of 398,000 acres of forestland in order to make disposable paper products for your kitchen and bathroom. How did it get permission for this kind of environmental pillage?

It hid its identity in a joint venture.

It paid off a trade association.

It "made friends" with government officials.

It bought the favor of tribal chiefs and local officials.

It even tried to bribe Equitanian environmental groups.

Unless we stop Vermilion now, it will flush more than 600 square miles of tropical rain forest down First World toilets. Then it will repeat the process in some other virgin place.

Let Vermilion Paper know how you feel about this exploitation of ecological treasures for gross commercial purposes. Write Oliver Hibbing, Vermilion's president and chief executive officer, and tell him what you think of his indifference to the people and forests of the world.

Originally Published in May–June 1991
Reprint 91311

About the Contributors

DAVID BIDDLE is Director of Research for the Center for Solid Waste Research, located in Philadelphia, and has more than 17 years of experience in the fields of energy and environmental planning for government, institutions, and business. He has published articles and editorials on environmental economics, technology management, and community development in numerous publications, including *Harvard Business Review, The Philadelphia Inquirer, Recycling Today, Philadelphia Business Journal, BioCycle,* and *Resource Recycling.* Mr. Biddle is a Contributing Editor to *In Business,* published by JG Press. He can be reached at Jango@aol.com.

STUART L. HART is an Associate Professor of Strategic Management at the University of North Carolina's Kenan-Flagler Business School. Previously, he taught corporate strategy at the University of Michigan Business School and was the Founding Director of Michigan's Corporate Environmental Management Program. Professor Hart's research interests center on strategy, innovation, and change. He is particularly interested in the implications of environmentalism and sustainable development for corporate and competitive strategy. He has published over 40 papers and authored or edited four books.

PAUL HAWKEN environmentalist, educator, lecturer, entrepreneur, journalist, and best-selling author, is known around the world as one of the leading architects and proponents of corporate reform with respect to ecological practices. He serves as a Cochair of TNS-International, a nonprofit educational foundation, and has founded several companies including Smith & Hawken, Datafusion, a knowledge synthesis software company, and several of the first natural food companies in the U.S. that relied solely on sustainable agricultural methods. He has served on the board of many environmental organizations including Point Foundation, Center for Plant Conservation, Conservation International, Trust for Public Land, Friends of the Earth, and the National Audubon Society. He is the author or coauthor of dozens of articles, scientific papers, and books, including *The Next Economy, Growing a Business*, and *The Ecology of Commerce. Growing a Business* became the basis of a 17-part PBS series which Mr. Hawken hosted and produced.

AMORY B. LOVINS is the Cofounder and Co-CEO of Rocky Mountain Institute, an independent, nonprofit resource policy center. His current research focuses on transforming the car, real estate, electricity, water, semiconductor, and several other manufacturing sectors toward advanced resource productivity. He has received numerous awards and recognition, including six honorary doctorates, a MacArthur Fellowship, the Heinz and Lindbergh Awards, and, along with his partner L. Hunter Lovins, the Nissan, Mitchell, and Onassis Prizes. In the *Wall Street Journal*'s Centennial Issue, he was named as one of the 28 people most likely to change the course of business in the 1990s, and *Car* magazine listed him as the twenty-second most powerful person in the global automotive industry. He is the author or coauthor of several publications. His most recent books, *Natural Capitalism* and *Small is Profitable*, are forthcoming.

L. HUNTER LOVINS is the Co-CEO of Rocky Mountain Institute, an independent, nonprofit resource policy center. A member of the California Bar, she cofounded, and for six years was Assistant Director, of the California Conservation Project (Tree People). She was the Henry R. Luce Visiting Professor at Dartmouth College, and has taught at several other universities. Along with her partner, Amory Lovins, she has received numerous awards, including the Mitchell Prize, the "alternative Nobel Prize," the Nissan Prize, and the Lindbergh Award. She lectures extensively at venues such as the World Economic Forum at Davos, consults for corporations and communities, and has coauthored nine books, including her most recent, *Natural Capitalism.*

JOAN MAGRETTA is a consultant and writer based in Cambridge, MA. A former partner at the management consulting firm of Bain & Company, she is a Contributing Editor of the *Harvard Business Review,* and winner of the McKinsey Award for 1998. Her latest book, *Managing in the New Economy,* is a collection of *Harvard Business Review* articles.

MICHAEL E. PORTER is the C. Roland Christensen Professor of Business Administration at the Harvard Business School, Cochairman, with Harvard colleague Jeffrey Sachs, of the Global Competitiveness Report, and a leading authority on competitive strategy and international competitiveness. He is the author of 15 books and over 75 articles. His books on strategy include *Competitive Strategy, Competitive Advantage,* and *On Competition.* His 1990 book, *The Competitive Advantage of Nations,* developed a new theory of how nations, states, and regions compete, and has guided economic policy throughout the world. In 1994, Professor Porter founded The Initiative for a Competitive Inner City, a nonprofit private sector initiative formed to catalyze business development in distressed inner cities across the United States. The holder of eight honorary doctorates, Professor Porter has won numerous awards for his books, articles, public service, and influence on several fields.

FOREST L. REINHARDT is an Associate Professor at Harvard Business School. His research concentrates on the relationship between environmental regulation and corporate strategy, the behavior of private and public organizations that manage natural resources, and the economics of environmental protection. He is the author or coauthor of several cases, articles, and books on the subject, including the book *Business Management and the Natural Environment*, with Richard H.K. Vietor, and his most recent book, *Down to Earth*.

ALISSA J. STERN is Founding Director of International Dispute Resolution Associates (IDR), a nonprofit organization aimed at developing the capacity of organizations to improve their ability to make decisions, prevent conflict, and resolve disputes. Current projects include a wide range of activities from creating an on-line collection of environmental organization–business collaborations with the Harvard Business School to bringing together youth leaders in Israel/Palestine, Cyprus, and Northern Ireland around local environmental initiatives. Prior to IDR, Ms. Stern was the Program Director at the National Institute for Dispute Resolution where she initiated the Institute's environmental and international programs and helped create a mechanism for the organization to become financially self-sufficient. Previously, Ms. Stern practiced environmental law at the law firm of Morrison and Foerster, consulted multinational institutions operating in Indonesia on environmental regulations, and taught environmental dispute resolution at the University of Indonesia Law School. Ms. Stern has published in the *Harvard Business Review*, *Harvard International Law Journal*, and *Environ-*

ment Risk (a Euromoney publication), and is currently writing a book on environmental collaborations.

CLAAS VAN DER LINDE is an Associate at the Institute for International Management Research (FIM) of the St. Gallen Graduate School of Economics in Switzerland. His primary research and consulting focuses on international and regional competitiveness and competition, as well as on issues of international management. He is the author of the book *Deutsche Wettbewerbsvorteile* (*German Competitive Advantage*) and author or coauthor of numerous articles in professional publications.

NOAH WALLEY is a Vice President of Morgan Stanley Dean Whitter, and is also a Vice President of MSDWVP, Inc., located in the New York offices of Morgan Stanley Dean Whitter. Prior to these positions, he focused on the telecommunications, technology, and environmental industries for the private equity firms of Bachow & Associates and Desai Capital Management, and also worked as a consultant for McKinsey & Company. In addition to his work at MSDWVP, Inc., he serves as a Director of Business Development Services, Osprey Systems, Inc. and Total Network Solutions, Inc.

BRADLEY WHITEHEAD is Cofounder and Managing Partner of CoreResources, an organization focused on providing management support and environmental services to promising, early stage companies with financially competitive, environmentally sustainable technologies. He is also the Founding Partner of McKinsey & Company's Environmental Practice, where he has worked with a broad array of companies to identify and capture environmental growth opportunities. In addition to his environmental work, he has nearly 15 years of experience in marketing, strategy, and operations research. He has also led an effort on public/private partnerships for the President's Commission on Environmental Quality. Prior

to working at McKinsey, Mr. Whitehead worked for the
National Westminster Bank in London, as an anthropologist
among the pygmies of Zaire, in the Brazilian Amazon, and as
a policy analyst for the Alliance to Save Energy. He chairs the
Environmental Advisory Committee of the Progressive Foundation and is Vice President of the Cleveland FoodBank.

Note: *Information provided within each article about the contributors
to case studies was applicable at the time of original publication.*

Index